MW01235046

Triumphant Over My Enemies: My Story. My Words.

A Mormon's Navigation Through
Same Sex Attraction to the Temple

By Keith Ivy, RN

ISBN_9781973235309

Published by SMOKEBLOOD Publishing
Casper, WY | smokebloodpublishing.com

Cover design and layout by Keira Faer
Cover design © Keira Faer, 2017
Edited by Keira Faer | keirafaer@gmail.com

Printed in the United States

To Brenda: my eternal companion, who was *truly* saved by **God** for me.

He knew what kind of companion
I would need in order to make a
successful Temple Marriage.

And To Nina, my sweetie pie cousin, whom I will never forget meeting for the first time at thirteen years old under the hair dryer.

She has always believed in me, and I will always love her for that.

CONTENTS:

"...I saw a pillar of light exactly over my head, above the brightness of the sun, which descended gradually until it fell upon me. It no sooner appeared than I found myself delivered from the enemy which held me bound. When the light rested upon me I saw two Personages, whose brightness and glory defy all description, standing above me in the air. One of them spake unto me, calling me by name and said, pointing to the other, *'This is My Beloved Son. Hear Him!'*"

- Joseph Smith, *History 1: 16-17*

Joseph Smith has always been my hero, of sorts.

While unjustly held prisoner in a fourteen square-foot dungeon at Liberty Jail during the winter of 1838-1839, and after suffering the horrible conditions of hunger, sickness and cold, Joseph Smith was spoken to by the Lord, who told him thusly: how no one has suffered as much as Jesus did when He was crucified and entombed; that the trials we face are for our betterment; and that, if Joseph would endure his well, God would exalt him on high, and he would **triumph over his foes**.

I have always loved that. Since I have, in no true way, suffered similarly, I know that I am strong enough to deal with whatever comes my way. Especially in dealing with those who may be cynical, because they haven't experienced the ups and downs in life that I have. But, that's me getting ahead of my story! Just get ready, sit back, and hold on tight to your Ava Gabor wig!

FOREWORD

By Laura Phillips

Keith is engaging. He draws you in. You can't help but want to know him - to know everything about him. And he will tell you - everything.

Keith likes to keep you off-balance. His teasing humor keeps you on your toes one minute, and then his warm-heartedness invites you to sit down for a heart-to-heart the next. He wants to take care of you and feed you lunch one minute, and then confide something unexpected the next.

The only rule in knowing Keith is… there are no rules. He wants everyone to be comfortable around him, yet ready to exchange ideas and stories at a second's notice. He's eager to discuss politics and religion, and to hear your thoughts, but antagonism and diversity have no cost with him - he welcomes them like old friends. His journey seems to be one of experience, learning, and gathering up; and whether he is gathering friends, ideas or stories - he's always collecting.

I remember the first time I met Keith. I had just begun a new job at a hospital far from home, and he was sitting at the break room table when I came in. Handsome, fit and smiling, he introduced himself. His voice was low and soft; almost velvety. His grin was infectious, and I was hooked.

Over the next months, when we worked together, he would share things about his life and family, revealing himself bit by bit. I can't say that I am especially perceptive, but I knew there was more to Keith and his life's story than, by his first presentation, was evident. He just has a soft demeanor; not overtly effeminate, but still there. I sensed it and he knew it.

Then one day he just straight up told me: he'd lived a life as a homosexual for many years, and had been as happy as he thought he could ever be. But, there was this thing, this knowledge, this foundation that would not be ignored. He had had a faith in God that was working on him - showing him the life he could have. It was this paradigmatic life that his Mormon faith had nurtured him in: an eternal life with a wife and children, where he would be present with them and his Heavenly Father forever, enjoying the blessings he'd received while in the Earthly realm. He couldn't ignore the calling.

When I first met Keith, he was already on the back side of that life-altering journey, and was proud of the life he'd built. He loved to tell the story about how Brenda was created just for him, how she'd waited just for him and how, having told her about his life before their meeting, she felt assured that he was her eternal soul mate.

He crowed about his son, who had been born the same week as mine and coincidentally shared the same name. He worked two jobs, so Brenda could stay home. He was the spiritual leader of his family in every way, making sure to attend church in their ward and to be an active part in building the church through charity and hard work. They looked forward to welcoming a second child. It took more than a year, but when their baby arrived, everyone knew that Keith and Brenda were in heaven on Earth.

Then Brenda got sick. Months of worry - terror, really - went by with Keith overwhelmed by the whirlwind of chaos that had become his life. How he made it through such a worrying time with that toothy grin on his face astonished us all.

But, again, there was more to Keith's life than met the eye, and more trials and tribulations lay ahead. Just how he made it through the storm is no small miracle in itself, but he did - he and Brenda did! Through all of this, Brenda may be counted as the biggest hero, as it was a journey for her, too - though a very different one. They each had to rely on their foundation of faith in God, what they know to be true scripturally, and an astonishing ability to forgive.

Keith and I are night nurses. We often talk late at night, during breaks when our hospital shifts become quiet and there is a natural lull that accompanies reflection. I am fascinated by the Mormon religion. Unlike my Baptist religion, it teaches that Christ loved and died for everyone, excluding no one from eternity. Keith has helped me understand their views about hell, sin and forgiveness, and so much more. Perhaps our late-night talks have strengthened my faith, and encouraged me to be more confident in where I am spiritually. I appreciate the struggles he has gone through, and challenge myself by confessing that if he and Brenda can survive and thrive after such a journey, then my walk has been easy.

I find it so exciting to have someone so willing expose himself and his religion to the tough questions of life: why we make the decisions we do, and why we follow this path and not that one, or change directions all together. I think we challenge each other at every level, and our friendship has been a gift. I look forward to every one of our conversations - no matter how short.

In the end, Keith's story is a one of redemption through the perseverance of faith: one we could all take.

I hope the reader is able to release the judgement we are all predisposed to with stories that seem almost outside the realm of what is normal, and see Keith's story for what it is - one man's journey through several phases of life that have created him on the way to where he is now. Perhaps, there is no one part more important than the other, but each is a piece of a puzzle that, though the picture is becoming more and more complete every day, is still being put together, and won't be completed until eternity is gained.

Though our religions may have different names, the goal is the same: to seek a more personal relationship with God, so that we might spend eternity with Him.

INTRODUCTION
Why I'm Writing…

The truth is a funny, fickle thing. One where so we often find

ourselves caught in the crosshairs; our fates left up to the opinions

of others. The only real way to carry on through these trials is to

know, in your heart, who you are and what you believe in.

My life has been a real rollercoaster. And as I delve quite deeply

into some of the more uncomfortable details, and bare my story to

not only my extended family, my children, and all of you readers,

but most especially to my wife, I hope for my words to make an

impact.

I hope, in crafting this book, for my story to make a difference in

the lives of others. I hope for you to find some inner guidance through my experiences, as well as, perhaps, some intrigue into the strange places my life journey has taken me.

This story is about remaining positive and pressing on. I hope for my story to inspire my children to dedicate themselves to the path that feels most authentic for them, individually. I want my children to know where to turn for help with the trials of their own lives, as they should arise. I hope for them to find solace in the same place as I have; namely, in the light of the restored gospel.

I hope for my story to inspire the same in all children of God, our Heavenly Father. Though the path may be ragged, and even though it may very well drag you through the mud and spit you out the other end, so long as you remain dedicated to who you really are, and navigate every trial that comes your way, you will find your way back to the truth; back to love.

Now, as you read on, remember that these are *my* experiences. My perceptions; my lessons learned.

I am in no way trying to tell you how you should live. If anything, my story proves how you can truly be anything, and how, so long as you persevere and stay true to your journey, you will find peace and love at the other end. So long as you remain in God's grace, and remember the unending love He has for you, you can combat any trial on the pathway toward finding yourself, and figuring out who you are.

I am currently a married man with two children, but I have embodied many other personas as I've made my way through this life. As you journey through my life story with me, remember to exert patience - the same patience we all must find within ourselves, in order to allow for our truest natures to arise. I have done some things in my life that may be perceived as shocking, but then, shock is subjective to experience.

A lot of events happened last year that brought my wife and I, and our children to Utah quite unexpectedly. I guess the Lord has a way of blessing us in unexpected ways, because being here has been exceptionally better than ever before. That's one of the reasons I am telling my story.

I came to realize that the lifelong attitudes I'd held for my relatives were in error, and should have, perhaps, been corrected years ago. But, that's what life's about I guess. Purge, realign and press on! I don't expect for anyone to agree with my life and actions. But then again, I have never wasted my time worrying about what anyone else thought of me. I am strong enough to handle my own life, and in the following pages you will find out why.

Additionally, I've come to realize recently that no one in my extended family ever *really* knew me, or even asked about my life. If they had asked, they would have understood me better, and they would have gained a point of reference for one of their own, who will likely lead a similar life. Good things have come from leaving what I can only call a destructive group of people.

I can't say that I wasn't warned. I just couldn't see it at the time. But, I'm getting ahead of the story.

First and foremost, I am a sixth generation Mormon. I am a Latter-day Saint. These purveyors to my personification have shaped who I am. Something in the subtleties of myself tells me they were aspects of my definition before I was born into this life. My steady faith in the LDS church seems to stem from my pre-existence; from when I was with God.

That's what Mormons believe: that we lived with our Father in Heaven before we came here with our families for our mortal probation. After that, our goal is to live with Him again, hopefully in an eternal family to receive His blessings; or rather, all that we are willing to receive. If you don't want to exert yourself through the trials that come your way, and don't want to overcome the struggles you're faced with to receive God's blessings, that is your choice. In the Mormon religion, there is no punishment for such things. Rather, you end up a bit less fulfilled, and instead of receiving the glory of God and all His blessings, you are given what will make you happy. But when you do not face something, it may continue to haunt you until you do, in some form or another.

Mormons believe that all people can be saved through Christ's atonement on the cross. We continuously try to live a life that honors this atonement, while spreading Christ Consciousness throughout the world with our thoughts and actions. When we sin, so long as we dutifully and justly repent, Jesus will forgive us. We acknowledge that we are not without sin, and that sin is the absence of the Holy Spirit. In opposition to other established religions, the sins we commit are lamps, lighting the road ahead, rather than blockades in the road. We are never without hope.

Those who may identify as same sex attraction, bisexual, gay, or lesbian can make and keep their covenants with God, as well as participate fully in the Church. Experiencing the attraction is no sin in the eyes of the Mormon faith, but sex outside the bonds of marriage is [regardless of gender choice] viewed as a hinderance to our eternal progress, and violates one of our Heavenly Father's most vital laws. With repentance, any who violate the law of chastity can be reconciled with God.

The Mormon faith does not allow man and man, or man and woman, to unite in a Sacred Temple Marriage. To be sealed as an eternal family in the LDS Church, I knew I would have to align myself with the pathway that led to the Temple. I knew I would have to traverse my trials, in order to find light along that path. I never felt guilty about my situation, nor about myself in general. I am me. Like it or not. I just realized and knew that by staying in that vein, I wouldn't get to where I wanted to go.

Since we all sin, we need a mediator or Savior to - if we believe in him and love him - pay the price for those sins on the cross. If we refuse, we have to pay the price for those sins ourselves - something we would hate to do since it caused even Jesus so much mental and physical pain in the Garden of Gethsemane to bleed from every pore. Thus, we embrace repentance and a conviction not to repeat the same mistakes.

I have never considered myself 'gay'. I hate labels like that. I am *me*, and have different likes and dislikes. As far as I'm concerned, these labels, such as 'gay', 'addict', 'alcoholic', and similar are just things you carry with you. These are the things you have to overcome in order to receive certain blessings from God. My father was a very good man and loved me. He also struggled with alcoholism. My mother, I think, struggled to accept her son as he was. We are all born into this life of trials. It is in overcoming our trials that we find ourselves closer to our Father in Heaven.

Same sex attraction is a very complicated thing. So many elements come into play when it comes to living this lifestyle. Every person you ask would give you a different answer for why and how they came to find themselves identifying as same sex attraction. I think most, nowadays, would simply say, *I was born this way*.

However, if I am to believe that Joseph Smith saw what he said he saw in the Sacred Grove, and heard the Lord speak, as I know he did, then there must be an explanation for same sex attraction that does not conflict with the Lord's Plan of Salvation. I could no more deny the story of Joseph Smith, than I could deny that Brenda is my wife. The church is too much a part of me, and always has been.

And Y'all: Please do not write, email or text me something derogatory about Joseph Smith, no matter what you heard, or where you heard it. You would be about fifty years too late. I already know what's true.

For these reasons, I have always tried my best to remain calm and wait on the Lord to see if there were ever any changes I wanted to make in myself or my lifestyle. For, I knew that if any changes were to be made, He would help me realize it. However, I also always knew in my heart that any changes I wanted to make in my life were *my choice*, and that God would love me either way. I knew He was there to support me, and that I had the freedom to choose what to do.

I never struggled with my religion. I have always found comfort in the scriptures. I have always held a firm reliance in Our Lord, and in the Mormon faith. My sexuality, however, has always been an issue. Ever since I was young, I found myself attracted to the same sex. But then again, I was also attracted to the opposite sex. I feel that, for me, same sex attraction (SSA) - or really any attraction - is not a black and white choice.

Sexuality is a journey of self-discovery we all take. Some of us are working with more of a broad spectrum; others a narrower one, but we all make the journey through our intimate self-expression. What I am trying to say is that despite my SSA, I have always tried to strengthen my testimony through increasing my knowledge, rather than running away from religion so I could go do my thing and not feel guilty about it. I always stood firm in my faith, willing it to light my path.

But why do I even care? Why have spiritual things always been on my mind? They've been there much more often these days, and especially so since I've had kids. Perhaps this is a natural part of parenting, or getting older, or perhaps arriving more fully into the true nature of self. No matter the reason, these are my thoughts; these are my words: **this is my story**.

Sometimes, we hold onto an emotion, like disdain for our mother, fear of our father, or merely the emptiness of not being loved as we feel we should've been growing up. But our parents will never love us perfectly. No one can ever truly love us perfectly. God is the only one capable of such a love. It is in our imperfect, trying love that our true selves are found.

The key is to be open and humble to what the Lord has in store for us, so we can find out who we really are. If we are only ever proud and defiant, we receive nothing. A doubting Thomas wouldn't see sincerity if it was staring him in the face; wouldn't believe the truth no matter how it was told to him. I do not believe that going into heaven waving a big 'ol pride flag will get you in to see our Father. I really don't. And when that day comes, I want in.

We each suffer our own trials. When we persist through the struggles that call us out, we each unearth our own truths. The culmination of the lessons learned on the earth balance us all, and help us continue to grow and to challenge one another.

In nursing school, we had to write maddening critical thinking papers that always began with the phrase: *The purpose of this paper is...* In thinking about my purposes for writing this book, I would register them in this order:

1. I want my wife and kids to know *me*, along with all I went through to become a Father and Husband. Additionally, and above all else, I want them to know that I understand and believe in the restored gospel of Jesus Christ as found in the Church of Jesus Christ of Latter-day Saints.

2. I hope others who experience same sex attraction will use my experience in obtaining their goals in life, if they so desire.

3. The struggle against evil is never over, so long as we are on this earth. The adversary will always try to knock you off your game when you are trying to keep your covenants, so stand firm in your faith, always.

4. I want to communicate that, no matter if you are gay or straight, Mormon or Catholic, black or white... lift up your head and rejoice! You are known personally to our Father in Heaven and His Son Jesus Christ, and they are available to help us with our goals in life.

CHAPTER ONE

Early Life: February 13, 1961 in Memphis – Crenshaw

My folks were both from North Mississippi, and initially lived on separate farms in Sarah and Crenshaw, Mississippi, respectively. My father's family have all been members of the Latter Day Saints (LDS) Church for over one hundred years in Mississippi. His family initially found the religion straight from the source, back when the early missionaries would still travel to find followers.

All that the followers of the church had back then was The Book of Mormon and a Bible; there was no formal Sunday School or education outside of the given literature. That is, until a man named Castleberry moved there from Texas, and brought with him literary teachings of all kinds. They were still baptized way back in those early days, however; just as my mother was when she married my father.

My mother still fits her high school photo: beautiful with translucent skin and only a few wrinkles. Her family was Southern Baptist, but when she married my father at nineteen, she grew determined to become a Latter-day Saint, unified with my father and his beliefs. Just as well, she was best friends with my father's sister at the time, my Aunt Sue. I'm sure that their connection had built within her a love for the faith as they attended high school together. Mother was really the one who kept us active in church throughout the family years.

Once my parents were old enough, they moved off the farm, and went to Memphis for work. My father, George, worked on a riverboat, on a barge on the Mississippi river in his late teens, and into his early twenties. My mother, Martha, was a secretary up until the time when she became pregnant with me, her first born.

I was born in Memphis, Tennessee, in the early spring of 1961. I arrived screaming into the same Methodist Hospital on Union Avenue where I would later attend the worst nightmare of my life: Nursing School [cue ominous music]. There is a special place in *hell* for nursing instructors. Just kidding…

My mother, Martha, became a stay-at-home-mom a few years after I was born. Then, only eighteen months later, my brother Kurt was born, solidifying her official stance as a stay-at-home parent. A few years on and Mitch and Chad were born, and she soon found herself overwhelmed with masculine energy, I'm sure.

Around this time, my father took up work with the Delta Oil Refinery in Memphis. I always thought that was a cool job. One of the perks was filling up your gas tank right at the refinery and logging the gallons in a notebook based off of the honor system! And though the honor system is now dead, my memories are not.

I so clearly recall the classic Ford Falcons that my parents had always driven. That was always their staple car: an old Ford Falcon with no air conditioning and a creaking straight shift on the steering column. So practical, even if it did smell a bit like the plastic the floors were made of. The first falcon we had was green; the second, gold. I remember when my brother Kurt and I were little, we could fit inside the actual steering wheel, and so we would rock back and forth there without end, laughing and giggling together!

I was always a sensitive child. Though I ended up the eldest of four boys, I was the least masculine. Of course, I was also the best looking of the lot, without a doubt! I used to get yelled or poked at from time to time by my mother for crossing my legs, or acting in some way that wasn't necessarily masculine. But my inherent sensitivity is a point of ponderance for me. A sort of chicken or the egg type scenario. Was I born super sensitive, or did I become that way as a result of my upbringing? I mean, who's to say, really?

I have to believe that I was not born into my same sex attraction. The other option is that my attraction was a result of my upbringing. Again, if I am to believe in the plan of salvation, there has to be another explanation other than just being "born that way". Sort of like formal logics. If A, then B. If *not* A, then *not* B. I was the arrow shot into the sky by my parents and their limitations. I do struggle with the blame, and try my best not to exert such egoist perspectives... but I wonder.

I feel that my calm, easygoing nature may have had the adverse effect of scaring my mother; bringing about an opposition in her mind, so that she didn't know how to approach my deviations from the norm. I mean, who could blame her? She was a young mother with four boys, and bills, and a husband who liked to escape the daily grind. Although I can pinpoint several events that most likely led to my eventual retreat from her attention, I still loved her every minute, and embracingly love her still. She is my mother, after all, and I see now that having me for a son must have been quite a trial for her.

Sometimes I think that I pushed away from my mother, perhaps, because I sensed her frustrations; perhaps, for other reasons. Regardless of what it all was, I love her, and I want to make it clear that I do not judge anyone associated with my upbringing.

I try to love and forgive all people for their imperfections, just as I try to forgive all trespassings. I commit myself to this life, in the hopes of claiming the atonement of Christ, who makes intercession for us to the Heavenly Father, for our shortcomings. Further, I have far too much garbage clogging up my life already, without adding "judge" to my title. And though this can be difficult to do on a regular basis; difficult to embody, I remember how Satan is the accuser, and that we must pardon one another, in order to receive our fair judgement from others when we trespass.

While in Memphis, my family lived in the typical post-World War II cracker box house: a three-bedroom, frame building with linoleum and hardwood floors, and only *one* bathroom [of course]. My father was very happy during this time: happy with work, happy with his home life, and happy to be around us kids.

Between my mother's confusion in how to parent me, and my father's overall jolly nature as I was a kid, I found myself consistently more drawn to him. His acceptance of me for my true self was something I recognized. His love was less contingent; less conditional. He was kind, even when he'd had a bad day.

One thing I wonder about is whether my love for my father had some sort of direct correlation to my same sex attraction. This could be one possible connection, as well. It is my belief that we are born pure, with a clean slate, and that our environment changes us, causing us to desire differently. [I cannot even entertain the contrary.]

Thus, I am led to believe that my SSA is the result of my upbringing. Not to say that same-sex attraction is a choice, however. I know firsthand how tempting same-sex attraction can be. Only, were we born attracted to the same sex, the entire concept of eternal marriage, the Temple rituals, and everything else that we ceremoniously entertain would be false. And that is impossible, because I know that what I have been taught is the truth. That it's just the way it is.

In my own story, I had to figure out how my sexual desires would or wouldn't fit into my life. No matter what I went through, felt, or tried, I was always comfortable with myself and the skin I lived in. I felt so comfortable under the warm, bright light of God's love that I knew, in every moment, I was loved and supported, no matter what. No matter what my instincts desired; no matter where my life experiences took me, I was loved and would be forever. I had only to figure it all out, and try my best to traverse my own trials.

Even my earliest of memories are shrouded in a sense of this awareness. I was so sensitive; so hyper-aware to what was going on around me, and even at such a young age as two or three, I can recall such clarity in my observations. I was always so attuned to what was happening in church and at school, aware of myself, receptive to the "talks" in church, and sensitive to the reactions of others when they met me. However, the feeling of security in regard to the restored gospel went onwards with me through life, supporting my sensitivities with strength.

Over the years, I've read letters that my mother wrote about me. One of the letters I found read,

Oh, Keith doesn't like to play outside much; he likes to cut and paste things.

Yes, it's true that I didn't like to play outside too much, and that I really wasn't all too masculine of a kid. But one thing I see now, that I couldn't see so clearly then, is that my sensitivity is a superpower. We are all given gifts, and we are, each of us, faced with opposition as a result of these gifts that set us apart from the masses.

When I was about four years old, my brother and I spent this one afternoon playing with toys under the kitchen table as my mother did the dishes. We were goofing around under there, as little kids do, pushing our toy trucks around and getting in car collisions, when I glanced up and saw the underneath of my mother's dress. Naturally, I was curious, so I leaned over a bit to see what was all under there.

As soon as she saw what I was doing, she freaked out. She tapped me on the head as if I had made some big mistake, when, truly, I had no idea what I was doing. I was only a curious child, after all. But, I can understand how she would worry. How she wouldn't know what to do in that situation. It is funny how these memories come back, sticking out; resurfacing as the stream of memories plays out in your mind.

I just really don't think my mother knew how to handle me as a kid. Perhaps, her actions stemmed from preset stereotypes from her own childhood. I did find out, in my teen years, that there had been an elderly gay man living in the small town where she grew up. Though she didn't go into any more detail about it, I can only imagine what the other townsfolk said about the poor guy. Especially back then. When I first learned about the "homosex'ul", as my grandmother called it, it hit me like a ton of bricks. I figure my mother may have associated my behaviors with the stereotypical features the old man was claimed to have had.

Sometimes I got scolded for "crossing my legs like a girl" when I was young. Though, all I thought I was doing was relaxing naturally. Funny how times change. Now, you go to any trendy spot in a contemporary city, and it's nearly impossible to tell who is on which side of the fence… or if there even *is* a fence. Such a scolding would be rare in today's climate. But don't even get me started on that!

Another scolding that I received was from my teachers at my elementary school in Memphis: Westwood Elm. When I was only in the first grade, my teachers would tell me off for choosing to stay inside and play, rather than go outside to get all dirty. They knew I was different, and they knew they didn't know what to do with it, so they scolded.

I was a bit embarrassed when stuff like this would happen, don't get me wrong, y'all. Just, my instinct wasn't to act differently or feel bad about it. Perhaps this is part of what made me different.

At home, I remember putting extra time into keeping my room clean. [You have heard the joke about the gay burglars? They break in and rearrange the furniture.] Well, I was always hoping to avoid a scolding. This motivated me to keep as clean as possible.

I was searching for solace, in those early years. I remember the joy I felt at attending church, and how comfortable I felt as myself. The church was in its infancy, and there really weren't too many Latter-day Saints there at the time, but I recall always loving it.

I so looked forward to going to church; especially in contrast to what things were like for me at home. Church seemed familiar to me, even at an early age. I felt embraced by the warmth I met there. And all I wanted, really, was to be able to be myself, and not be bothered about it!

So, the church was always there for me; God was *always* there. I remember watching shows like *December Bride* or *I Love Lucy* on our little black-and-white TV. Instead of football or sports, I would always choose these sitcoms. Luckily, my own father wasn't into sports, or at least, he didn't push it on me at all. He was always willing to spend time with me, doing things that he knew I would enjoy, or at least get something out of; especially so in those early years.

Another memory that sticks out to me with absolute clarity is from when I was in first grade. I was always wanting more attention, and always held secret hopes of being more special and incredible than all the other children. I mean, I guess maybe all kids feel this need; and perhaps it isn't *so* uncommon, but it seemed essential for me back then!

One day in class, I overheard the teachers discussing this one student. He was being moved to a different section - what was in my mind an obviously better section - due to the fact that: *Well, he just needs a change.*

I was immediately upset at that kid for getting extra attention!

I wanted it, and so I started to weave a little web to get myself moved into the same section. I started kissing up to the teachers and doing better in all my work until they decided to move me. How interesting, what a little motivation can do!

As I got older, I started to recognize there was something different about me. Something in my character that stood out against the backdrop that was everyone else. I think my mother knew it too. She had always known, and perhaps had been tormented by what she knew.

Throughout my entire home life and all through high school, I remember seeing my mother on her knees by the bed praying each night. Our house was situated in a way where us kids had to go through my parents' room to get to the bathroom, and I would always see her there, perfect as a prayer card. I imagine I could've easily been the subject of some of those prayers.

After my third brother, Mitch, was born in 1968, our family moved back home to Mississippi, where both sides of my extended family resided. My father had five siblings there, and my mother four. I felt so excited after we moved back to Mississippi, to live within a few miles of both sets of grandparents! Everyone was so close at that time; there was such a prevalent sense of family.

Each and every Sunday, my family would go to my mother's parents' house. My grandma Willie was the *best* cook the Lord ever did put on this Earth, and I loved her very much. My mother's father, DD [as we called him], was a farmer in the Mississippi Delta all his life. After growing up and moving away, I have often kicked myself for not riding on that tractor with him at least once.

Grandma Willie worked as an elementary school lunchroom lady. She never learned how to drive, in all her life. She had a very strong sense of will. It was often difficult to change her mind once she'd made it up. I loved smelling DD's cigars when I was a kid. He always seemed so happy; always jingling the coins in his pockets, and whistling as he walked. Willie and DD raised their five kids in the Mississippi Delta, and taught them all to be self-sufficient and strong, just like them.

I found myself a bit closer with my father's side of the family growing up. This may be partially due to the fact that my father's parents were Mormon, just like I was, and I saw them at church on Sundays. We were all a part of that community together. Also though, when we were at my mom's folks' place, there really weren't any other kids around; whereas, at my dad's folks', there was always so much to explore and get into with the cousins, and just so much more for us kids to do in general.

Each time all of us cousins were together at my Grandma Irene's (father's side), we would search the barnyard for dead animals to bury in our animal graveyard. We would sing a primary song all together, and have a little service for the deceased. Funny stuff.

CHAPTER TWO

Grade School: 7 Years Old - Eighth Grade

In moving back to the rural setting of Mississippi, and living so close to family on both sides, I started to find my solace and self-confidence a bit more. I began the second grade there in Crenshaw, at Crenshaw Elementary, and stayed there for a couple years.

I didn't necessarily have many friends in grade school, and I still felt a bit different from most kids I met. I knew that my inherent tendencies and lack of athleticism may have been somewhat to blame for my lack of friends early on in school, but I wasn't all too worried about it at the time, to be honest. I was bullied here and there. You know how it is: if you're not the bully, then you're probably being bullied. I did have a few friends here and there, and was definitely drawn to other kids that didn't quite fit into the mainstream either.

I made many more friends at church - as I really did use it as a refuge - and, as well, saw cousins, spent time with my grandparents, hung out with my siblings, and even bonded in some ways with my parents. I was by no means lonely, and overall, it was a much better atmosphere for me than living in Memphis.

My family was lucky enough to have a ward (Mormon congregation) in Mississippi at the time, where we would attend church. I really settled into it, soaking up the gospels as I heard them. I loved singing the songs about "going to the Temple", and was inspired by the scriptures. I just felt good at church. I had friends, and everyone was so supportive.

I felt an extreme sense of belonging, which, really, gave me the foundations to figure myself out.

I was pretty confused at the time. Early on, I knew only that I was somehow a little different than the other kids. Eventually, I did realize that I was less masculine than most of the boys. Then, around puberty, I had this moment of reckoning, where I connected non-masculinity to being gay. I thought, because I wasn't masculine, it must mean that I was gay. Of course, after I moved into the real world, I saw that this was not even close to true. But back then, I was pretty convinced.

When I realized that I was gay, or at least SSA, I wasn't upset about it. I just kinda shrugged at life, and thought to myself that if that was the way I was, that was okay. I knew I was loved by the Lord, and didn't care to judge or alienate myself, as a result. Although I knew it would be difficult for me to progress to the Temple if I acted on my feelings, I also knew in my heart that if I wanted it, I would be able to figure it all out someday.

I knew what was happening, but I didn't really feel badly about myself as a person. I think that confidence and self-love was all due to my Mormon faith. I often hear of the guilt and self-hatred people walk around with for being the way they are, and I am grateful to my religion for teaching me about my eternal worth as a person; as a Child of God. I knew I'd figure it out someday, if the Temple was what I wanted. And it was.

When we first moved, my father had planned on building a new house for our family, but then at the last minute, he decided to purchase an older house with more land. And when I say old, I *mean* old: it was pretty rough, and there was no running water. We had, instead, a cistern that sat underneath the house and ran up into it, from which the former owners would draw out water. It was like this for us for a short while, up until my handyman of a father decided to install a modern water pump system in the house. Around the same time, he worked to rewire the electricity and put on a new roof.

I remember driving up to that house for the first time and seeing the huge mimosa trees that strung themselves all the way around the property. The small house sat on five acres of land that my mother still owns to this day. Scattered about the land, you would find persimmons, wild plums, and huge chestnut trees.

As I was already paying mind to decorative, ornamental things at the time, I vividly recall the pattern of linoleum that ran along the floors in our house. There were all these different colored linoleum squares that, when combined, made a pattern; a design that I thought was pretty unusual and interesting.

The lady who had lived in the old house before we bought it was named Evelyn, and I only mention her because she is absolutely worth mentioning. She was a highly talented Native American woman, who had kept all her crafts in these storage buildings that were strewn across the property. When she lived in the house, she used to create Shadow Boxes: framed images combined with feathers of all sorts, sometimes in the shape of a peacock or some similar bird, using bright, vibrant, beautiful colors to complement, that you would then hang on the wall. Our neighbors, the Floyds and Jennings, used to reap the benefits of her crafts. As I would be in their homes for one reason or another growing up, I noticed the shadow boxes she had crafted and given to them.

When my family first moved to the land, my brothers and I got to explore the area, including Evelyn's storage buildings. And oh, boy, the things we found in those buildings! There were hundreds of feathers, from all sorts of birds, in all sorts of colors and sizes; wicker baskets she must have used to collect her goods; and then we found all these Mason jars filled with locks of hair. Evelyn had cut and displayed locks of her own hair in all these jars on the shelves of her storage space. Whether she used the hair for something, or just didn't like to throw it out, I'm still not sure, but I remember speculating back then as to why she might have left it there!

In later years, we had livestock that we raised on the acreage, and there was this reservoir that the animals would all drink from. It was such a neat place to grow up, and especially so after living, at first, in the city. I remember the time Daddy built us a tree house! Definitely a change from city life.

We were able to roam free, and we were closer to our extended family than ever before. We spent time with my mother in the garden, pulling weeds and clearing the brush that grew up every so often. My mother was still a housewife at the time, and there were always chores for us to do.

My brother Kurt now lives in the house, and it has been remodeled several times over since my father originally bought it. Now, it's just an old farmhouse, relatively worn in years.

A railroad track runs straight through Crenshaw, and back in the sixties, the whites lived on one side and the blacks on the other. Even up into the early seventies, as I was attending grade school, the town was just beginning to integrate itself. The railway naturally segregated the town, to where blacks had their own stores on their side of town, and even though they would often come over to the side that I was living on, these things were all still in a state of transition. I remember, there was one movie theater in Crenshaw, where the black citizens would all have to sit upstairs; the whites downstairs.

Crenshaw sits just at the edge of the Mississippi Delta. To the east, the hills rise with lots of trees and green. To the South and West, it's all flat, Delta farmland. During the fifties and sixties, it was a thriving community with a huge cotton gin. Now, like so many small towns, industry has moved into the more populated areas, and only a small community remains, with one bank, one grocery store, and a hardware store.

We lived pretty close to the border of our county, and my grandparents (my dad's folks) lived just on the other side, so we were able to catch the school bus from their house more easily. Some mornings, my mother would drive us quickly to our grandparent's house before the bus came, and other days we would just spend the night there, and wake up to hop right on the bus. It was at that time that my grandmother, Irene Berry, had a wood stove she would light and use to cook breakfast for us, all the while telling us about the early life of her side of the family. She would tell us all about her thirteen brothers and sisters who had all joined the LDS church around the turn of the century.

Grandma Irene often bore her testimony to me about the church and what it would do in my life. She seemed to always have a positive attitude, and I loved her. Later on in life, we would get together and order things from the Spencer Gifts catalog. Once, we got a plastic owl to hang in the garden to scare away crows. Another time, I ordered her a personalized "chopper hopper" from there, with *IRENE* engraved on it, to keep her teeth in at night! Haha!

My grandfather on my father's side was named Edgar LaVerne Ivy. He and my father - together - built the house that my grandparents lived in at that time. They always kept a feather bed in their screened-in back porch, and in summers I would sometimes sleep back there with Granddaddy Verne. Many mornings, I would wake up to a chicken sitting on the footboard of the bed! I actually still own that land today, not that it's anything all too special, and have swapped ownership back and forth with my brother Kurt a bit over the years to keep it in the family.

I have so many ancestors from that side of the family who really gave their hearts to the gospel!

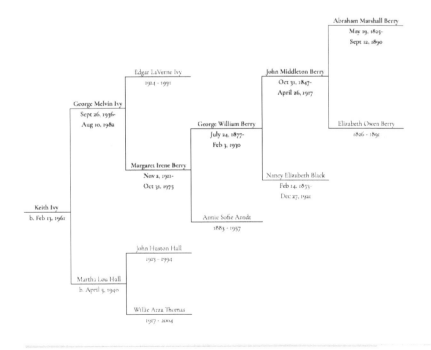

My 3rd great-grandfather, **Abraham Marshall Berry** (1825-1890) was the first person in my family to join the LDS church in Chickasaw County, Mississippi. The missionaries would travel through there every six to twelve months, teaching and baptizing. Around 1888, there was a group of anti-mormons living in the area. One time, when the missionaries came through, the anti-mormon mob was looking for them, obviously to cause them harm and expel them from the city.

Abraham and his wife hid the missionaries in their home.

Back then, some homes in the south had two living areas; one on each side of the house, with a breezeway going straight through the middle. From what I understand, Abraham was shot in the back while in the breezeway, sitting in his nightshirt, because the mob had found out that he was hiding the missionaries away.

His wife picked out the buckshot with a sewing needle, but the ball was too deeply embedded. Abraham contracted lead poisoning from the ball and, unfortunately, died about a year later, after fleeing to Provo, Utah. They were driven out of their home by the mob. His wife died soon thereafter, and they are both buried now in Provo Cemetery.

My grandmother was always telling us stories like this, and not just about the family, but about members of the church and those we'd grown up with. As a result, I found myself thinking,

Can I live up to what the people before me have gone through? My life is so easy compared to theirs. I'm not hunting and gathering. I don't drive a horse and buggy…. How will I show my true strength?

It seems as though I have been aware of spiritual things throughout my life. As such, I have established some absolutes regarding my purpose here. I only have to keep trying, to see if I can achieve the goals I have set for myself. To see if I can prove to the world around me - through my choices and my actions - the strength I have inside, no matter what trials and tribulations may come my way.

Mormons are well-known for their interest in genealogy, and mine is no different. We have such a large extended family, that we would - and still do, to this day - get together every other year for a massive reunion. We usually meet up at a campsite, and though it's no longer so large as it used to be [blame family planning, the natural diaspora, or whatever you like] there were scores of relatives in attendance at those reunions.

Though I do have such a large extended family, there are a few relatives who've always stood out; with whom I've forged special relationships over the years. One of these gems is my Aunt Wylodine - my father's eldest sister. We had always just called her "Aunt Dean", and she was ravishing: so beautiful and stylish. I loved her all my life, and always looked up to her. She came in once with some *hateful* two-tone pumps that I couldn't help but notice. [I know. Stop.] She just always looked great, and especially so to my fashionably interested mind. I mean, I'm sure I drove my mother crazy with my interest in such things, but that's just what I paid attention to at the time.

Wylodine lived in Shreveport, Louisiana, with her family. She would come up to visit every few months, and every time she did, I would do everything in my power to hang out with her, and really just be near to her in any way I could. I was quite drawn to women during that time, and especially so when they opened their hearts up to me.

Another one of those unique gems in my extended family is my cousin Nina. She's around eighty, and lives in Salt Lake City now, but I have a place in my heart for her, to which this book is dedicated. She and my Aunt Wylodine are basically the same age, and grew up together, playing, attending school, and such of the sort. The two girls used to leave notes for one another hidden in the bark of a tree, to communicate whenever they couldn't see each other. I loved hearing all their stories when I was growing up.

So anyways, my family had just settled into life on the land, spending more time with my grandparents and family, when my father decided to move us to Shreveport, where my Aunt Wylodine and Uncle Sonny lived. I was ecstatic because, naturally, I loved my aunt more than anything, and I wanted to be near her all the time. But of course, it's quite different when you don't see relatives that often, compared to when you live right there, smelling their sweat and seeing their lives unfold at your feet.

We only lived there in Shreveport for about a year and a half when my father moved us straight on back to our same house in Crenshaw. Basically, we moved to Shreveport late on in '72, and we moved out of there by the time 1974 rolled around. I think my father was just more comfortable in the country than in the city, and probably wanted his four boys to have a more rural homestead on which to grow up. While in Shreveport, I attended Oak Terrace Junior High. My father started to drink a bit more at this time, and there were problems with that, no doubt, but my mother was still a housewife in Shreveport, and it was a good experience overall while we lived there.

After we moved back, I was in the thick of it with puberty, attending junior high, and beginning to act a bit more on my feelings for both boys and girls. Of course, not in any incredulous way: I was still quite innocent in my desires and experiences, but I did test the waters, to be sure. And it was strange for me at times when we first moved back: going to school in the same town I had just left, and running into wayward members of the church and all that.

My best friend in middle school was named Donald Tanner. Come to find out, he and his family were members of the church! They were mostly inactive there, but Donald and I were thick as thieves. It was 1973, and some kids my age were wearing long hair, as did Donald. My dad wouldn't hear of it. I hated it, but it was probably for the best. Mine probably would have bushed out like Roseanne Roseannadanna's did on *Saturday Night Live*! Another blessing, right?!

CHAPTER THREE

High School: 9th Grade - Junior College

High school was a trip. I got to know myself better, and forged some quality friendships along the way. The school I attended was connected to the grade school my brothers and I had gone to in our grandmother's county. The demographic ratio was about sixty percent black and forty percent white. It was, quite frankly, a really good education, even if it was a 1970's Mississippi public school.

Even during this time, I would notice patterns and decorations; fashions and aesthetics. I would always look around during church to see if anyone was wearing shoes that didn't match their handbag, or something of the sort. Silly stuff. I just remember noticing, and being very observant about what people were wearing, as well as whether or not they should've been wearing what they were.

My best friend from eighth through twelfth grade, David, was black, and I recall all of our black teachers trying to break us up; encouraging him to find another friend. Others would make comments from time to time, as well, urging me towards finding a white friend instead. Of course, he and I didn't give a flip about what those folks thought or said, and remained best friends regardless. He was so accepting, and even though he understood my tendencies, was never bothered by such things.

I couldn't wait to get to school every day just to hang out with him! David and I would laugh all day every day, making offensive noises in class, and just having a blast together! Our teacher, Tommy Lacefield, was so enraged at times, because he couldn't - for the life of him - figure out who was making the noises! Outside of class, we would tape record ourselves laughing and goofing around, and then would play it back for ourselves and split our sides in laughter each time! He was such a good friend.

My grandmother Irene died on Halloween in 1975, and the night before, I had played Dracula in a haunted house. As I balled my eyes out the next day - because I couldn't get the black nail polish off my fingernails - David just sat there with me, scraping the polish off my hands as I cried.

At that time, people down south generally still brought the body home for the wake instead of holding it at a funeral home, so Grandma Irene's wake was held at my aunt Peggy's (my father's youngest sister). She lived in the coolest house; it reminded me of Frank Lloyd Wright architecture. Irene was only sixty-one when she passed. I'll never forget the pink gown and pink casket that she was buried in. She was beautiful. I still remember the song played at the funeral: *Sunday*, which I learned to play on the piano in later years.

Granddaddy Verne told me, after my grandmother had died, that he would amputate both arms to get her back, if he could. This put a smile in my heart, if not on my face…. He lived another seventeen years, bless his heart.

Around this time, my Mr. Fix-it of a Father installed a bird bath in our front yard. It was three-tiered, with a plethora of concrete sea-horses. One afternoon, my little brother Mitch [who was about three at the time] went outside, and began to swing on the birdbath. The concrete bowl came down on him and crushed his chest, collapsing one of his lungs. Mother and Daddy took him immediately to the hospital in Clarksdale, MS, where he barely made it. They had chest tubes and life support in place, and finally, after days and days, he recovered. My parents were distraught. I always remembered the special love my Dad had for Mitch. He would hang on his back, hands around his neck with feet in his belt, laughing.

My father, soon after, insisted that our family get a pig and a cow. *These boys* *need something to do besides work in a full acre garden*, he said.

I thought, *Lordy Mercy*!

Now, all that *really* meant was that my brother Kurt and I would have to milk the cow twice a day, year-round, from then on out. And let me just tell you, that as I spent those cold, wintry mornings getting slapped repeatedly in the face with an icy, feces-stricken cow tail, I wondered what the hell I was really doing there. I thought, *shouldn't I be on a dance floor somewhere?*

Studio 54 had just opened in NYC in 1976. *Lord, where is Andy Warhol?* Maybe that's where I should've been instead of with the ol' cow. That all lasted for about three years - all that milking - and then the cow died. I was sad outwardly, but on the inside, it was party time! I was doing ballet pliés and pirouettes all around the pasture, finally free! Free from my daily responsibilities, and free from stepping down, barefoot, into anymore steaming hot piles of cow poop!

My heart went out to that poor cow, though. Whenever we were late coming home, she would always be up at the fence, staring me down, her milk sack bulging along with her eyes, as though she were willing me to come closer and relieve her swollen udders.

Those years were all quite happy. I mean, there were of course a few episodes here and there, but nobody's childhood is perfect. And really, I was always an obedient teenager to my parents. I never partied, never got into any trouble, and always observed their rules.

My father seemed to always love me. I'm sure that he wrestled with my stuff, and maybe talked about it with his brothers and sisters, but to me he never showed a thing. When I was a senior in high school, I got a job working with my aunt Peggy, as a nurses-aid in Senatobia Hospital. I had made enough money, after a while, to buy my own stereo set and turntable that I kept in my room. One day, my daddy walked in, and I was in full spin around the room, with hair like *Welcome Back, Kotter*, dancing around to the Village People, or the score of *Showboat* [...I can't quite remember which, but it was always one of the two.]

Oh, *Lord*, what brain damage I must have caused. He was still standing as he said, *Well, keep going!* I politely declined, and mentally prepared myself to catch him if he fainted.

In the LDS church, we have what's called seminary, where we study the scriptures. The scripture study cycled through all four years of high school, moving from the study of the Old Testament, to the New Testament, the Book of Mormon, and then the Doctrine and Covenants. The course was taught as a home study, almost like a Sunday School class, and we would regularly meet on Sundays to discuss the scriptures. Then, it was the student's responsibility to work in the book and study the scriptures in some way each day throughout the week.

Usually, seminary is held in a building on the school's campus, but back in rural Mississippi, there were only a few of us Mormons in the whole school, so we would meet in the basement of our church - in the leaky, creaky basement. Whenever it rained, we would have to use brooms to push the water down the drains before getting down to business. Keith, Ricky, Cheryl and Robin… that was it, save for Miss Linda.

Our teacher's name was Linda Welch, and boy do I love that woman. She was beautiful, and I would just sit there and listen to her pour her heart out like a flowing river of scripture. The way she would bare her testimony about what we were studying, and how she would make connections, motivated and inspired me greatly. At the time, I was struggling a bit with self and sexual identity [really what teen doesn't], and even though I didn't feel guilty about it or anything, was really inspired by her testimony. Even later on in life, when I really started to pull things together for myself, I referred back to the knowledge and insight that she instilled in me so early on.

One passage I was particularly drawn to during this time was 1 Corinthians 2: 9-14. For example:

Eye hath not seen, nor ear heard; neither have entered into the heart of man, the things which God hath prepared for them that love him.

I didn't want to have limits placed on my eternal progression for any reason - especially my personal struggles.

High school summer trips were seminary trips. The Mormon Temple for the Memphis Stake [a stake is comprised of multiple congregations] was actually located in Washington DC back then, because there weren't all that many members. Now there's one in Memphis, as the following has grown so much over the years. One summer, we took a bus trip with all the other Mormon kids in the stake to check out the Temple in DC, and I just loved it. It was so great to just connect with other Mormon kids from the stake, and ride all together on a bus, goofing off and getting to know one another.

Like others my age, puberty brought about a plethora of new interests and desires. During high school, I really only went on three different dates with women. None of them went very well, because I felt weird and knew that something else was going on under the surface for me.

My first date was with a girl who played basketball and was taller than me. She was so tall they called her "Weiner." She was very pretty but I thought, *this feels so weird*. At the time, my hair was going through a phase, so she probably thought it was weird too.

The second date I had was with a knock-out. This beautiful girl with hair to her waist. I was a nervous wreck as we drove over to the Oxford to see *Saturday Night Fever*. I wanted to kiss her so badly, but as I basically looked like Waldo in the Van Halen video *Hot for Teacher*, I couldn't work up the nerve.

My third date was with my friend Cindy. We decided to go to the prom together! We had a great time, and after the prom we went with other classmates to a new Disco in Memphis called *Escapade*! Haha. I wore a two-toned terry-cloth shirt out that night… [I know... Stop... I told you I had a vivid memory.] Anyways, we had a great time that night, even though I knew something else was brewing.

With all this going on, I still had the desire to study what brought me comfort. I have always been a history buff, and it's just fascinating to witness the patterns of history repeated today. I really began to mature into the Word of the Lord during this time, and felt very comfortable in my own skin as I made my way through these experiences.

Besides those three dates I went on during high school, there was this one other girl. She was from Jonesboro, Arkansas, and was in our stake. I would always see her at the monthly Super Saturday gatherings of seminary students, and she was just so pretty. She had such a nice figure, and I was always enthralled. I remember that she just loved the band Chicago. She and I would talk a lot, and hold hands and all that, but it was right in the midst of my own inner struggle that I met her, and frankly, there was no way I was going to involve someone real in my life until I'd figured things out for myself first.

I remember in the eleventh grade, my younger brother found a risqué magazine that I had hidden. He tattled on me to my parents, so I waited and waited for their punishment to arrive. When, after a few weeks, nothing happened, I asked my mom what was up with that. She was not the type to let a lesson go unlearned. She said to me,

Oh, you know… just don't do it again.

Well, then I really knew something was up. I figure my folks must have been relieved to see women in that magazine instead of dudes, and just didn't want to discourage my interest!

When I was eighteen or nineteen years old, I went to see my Aunt Wylodine in Shreveport. That was the first time she seemed to sense something about me, and so she just looked at me and said,

I knew you would tell me.

She knew. I said, *I will figure this stuff out. I promise, but not now. I just can't.*

The years rolled on, and I became more confident as I got closer to graduation, about myself and what I was gonna do. One thing I've always aligned with, in my study of the gospel, is to treat others as you wish to be treated. Those who have had, and describe, near-death experiences, come back and say that how you treat your fellow man - and how you make him feel - is what's most important. If you make someone feel badly, and you never try to do anything to rectify the situation, then just like a fire-powered boomerang, those feelings will come back to you, most likely putting you in a situation that forces you to see, learn and understand that individual's side of things. I firmly believe that.

And quite frankly, I have enough garbage to deal with in my life, that I would never want to attract such things, and as a result I do not and will not go around waving my opinions of others in the air, as though I am somehow authorized to do so. I don't do that - never have - and that's a large part of what became ingrained through my study of the scriptures during this time.

With the encouragement of my friends, and the inspiration of Sister Welch, I tried to draw ever closer to my heavenly potential, and I never let my connection to the scriptures, nor to God, falter as a response to my teenage confusions and explorations.

CHAPTER FOUR
Memphis: 1980 – 1994

When I graduated high school in 1979, the first thing I did was sign up to attend Ole Miss (The University of Mississippi). However, my cousin and roommate at the time had talked me into going to Northwest Mississippi Community College in Senatobia with him for a year, first. While roommates with him, I registered [again] to attend Ole Miss that following year. I couldn't make up my mind yet on what to do for a career, though, so I registered for general studies.

I guess not too many of us really do know what we want at that age, anyways. Or, if we do "know", we may change our minds a bit as time moves forward, before really hunkering down and setting our minds to one thing. That age had always seemed to be, to me, more of an age for self-exploration. Then, once you've explored, you come to understand yourself enough to know how to best fold yourself into society, as well as enfold your life with another's.

I don't define myself by my struggles. I am me with different likes and dislikes. I wouldn't define someone who likes to drink as an alcoholic when I think of them, and the same for any other personality trait or desire. What I do define myself by is my Mormon faith. My faith in God and his love for me is the foundation of my existence. The knowledge I possess as a Mormon, regarding who I really am and why I am here on earth to begin with, makes me calm and nonjudgmental regarding any label that might be placed on me by modern society.

In the meantime, when I was attending Northwest Mississippi Community College, I knew I wasn't going to be able to avoid finding out more about the gay community. Being fresh off the farm, and still a bit immature in some ways, my curiosity compelled me: I just had to find out what was going on on the other side. I didn't necessarily struggle with the experiences, nor with the understanding that I was attracted to the same sex. I knew it was real - I accepted it - but I knew there was a reason for it: one that didn't conflict with what I already *knew* in my heart to be true.

One night, I was out with some friends. I'd been wondering where the gay club in town was, but hadn't been able to covertly find out any information. I tried to play it as cool as I could when asking around, since I was still unsure of how to act on that side of myself. Once I found it, and went inside, I just *loved* the music... oh, and the dance-crazed discotheques!

I felt some sadness there, in putting my religious desires on the back burner, but I still felt that someday I would figure that all out. In the Mormon religion, when you resist the temptations of the material world, you receive the Lord's blessings. Although I knew what I should do, I was still immature and wanted to figure things out for myself.

There was just no going around it, for me. My same sex attraction was overwhelming my attention at that time in my life. So, I knew I had to see what was going on, and follow through on those desires and impulses, in order to figure myself out. Like a gateway to my own understanding, I knowingly passed beneath it.

Partaking in my first relationship with a male was like crossing a threshold. I knew it was inevitable; I could feel it in my heart that I wanted it, but I could also feel in my heart that I would potentially lose out on some of the Lord's blessings by following through.

This moment of dissonance was defining for me. Because, at the same time, I knew who I was, and that the Lord loved me eternally and infinitely for that. I was confident in the fact that things were going to work out for me if the Heavenly Father willed it to be so, and thus, I held his love as the bridge that allowed me to move forward and explore this side of myself.

I knew I was loved, no matter what I was doing.

The thing about my first relationship was that we were less committed to one another in the traditional sense, as we both wanted to explore the dynamism of our youth. Plus, a part of me felt that if I kept myself out of a serious relationship with a guy, it would be easier to eventually find my way to the Temple. We didn't get too worked up about it, and rather, somewhat drifted apart after that first year.

This was how sexuality at the time was very much structured. Sexuality in the eighties was an open, free, variable experience - big hair and all. So, after a time, we stopped seeing one another and I moved in with some mutual friends of ours, settling myself into my new lifestyle in Memphis. I loved meeting others like me, with similar backgrounds or stories from their youth.

Of course, choosing this life came with its own challenges. Some in the community were dropping like flies around me in the eighties, and I bet you can guess why. One thing I think really saved me from contracting HIV or any other form of disease was how I was so connected with the church. I was never too promiscuous, never too rebellious, and never took to shaking a fist in the face of the church. Instead of outrage, I found peace.

Instead of saying, *Well, this is me, and to hell with everything else*, I enveloped a sense of patience with myself and what I knew about myself. I knew the understanding would arrive eventually, and that I would figure it all out in the end. I knew, if there was a better plan for me out there, I would find it when I was meant to. I trusted in the flow.

I honestly don't believe God is repulsed by two people of the same sex being together. At least, not any more than any other action that puts distance between us and our Heavenly Father. I don't think God - so loving and supportive as He is - could ever be forlorn over such things. I do know that his mercies were with me, even as I was exploring that side of myself. I know, in my heart, that my faith is a big part of what protected me during the AIDS crisis, and kept me healthy.

The thing is, you *have* to be humble. And, well, you can't be rebellious. Trust in life, and try your best. [And enjoy the ride!] Ride your life like a wave into the sunset. Find peace and serenity in your journey, and trust that whatever the currents may be, they will lead you to where you're meant to be. The Lord will guide the currents around you, and will carry you if you falter, so long as you believe in his presence and acknowledge his love. And so, that's what I did.

And boy, was Memphis a blast in the eighties. Such a youthful menagerie of celebration, love, and exploration. Crime was low, and everyone was keeping to their own business, all the while partying about it. The local bar, George's, had an incredible drag show, *Showcase of the South*, that kept no one away. Straight, gay, whatever: it was a good time. Those girls were just fabulous. Sunday afternoons at three o'clock, they held a tea party that flaunted the dancing talents of their female impersonators. And like clockwork, every Sunday, that place was packed!

Such a contrast to life milking that ol' cow.

I remember noticing how much work went into these shows and I enjoyed watching them. I would often try to think about those individuals and the lives they came from. I *knew* they were just as I: known to God. Those shows would go on for hours with songs from disco, Broadway, and comedy skits. They were definitely talented, and being new to the scene, I often thought of the contrast between what was happening before me, and the rural setting I had just come from.

When I first made the move to Memphis, I got a job working for the power company: Memphis Light, Gas and Water (MLGW). I worked in the billing office with all these lovely ladies. Some of them had been there for years, some of them were new when I was, and some of them I am friends with to this day. In a way, I grew up with them: they knew my story, knew what I was going through, and even knew all my friends. For eight years, it was a great place to work.

Those people saw me grow up, and witnessed... quite a bit more of my immaturity than I may like to admit. I was still really just finding my way at the time, and they were all so supportive, really. One of the ladies I worked with, Edna, just loved to listen to the black gospel station on the AM radio: WLOK [*Makin' it happen!*]. Small radios were just beginning to become common, so we would listen to her favorite songs daily. She absolutely loved the Lord, and every Monday morning she would walk up to my desk and ask,

Keith, did you go to church yesterday?

I would usually say, *No, I didn't.*

And then she'd say, *You went to the disco Saturday night, didn't you?*

...Stayed all night long, said I.

She'd respond, *What, you can't go to church after acting up the night before?*

Oh, I just loved her... loved our dynamic!

In the office, there were only a few male workers, and then otherwise it was mostly just women, and especially so mostly black women. You know, Memphis at that time was still in transition, though moving steadily forward, so it was still a bit of a "thing" to be friends with only black women if you were white. That tension was still being tugged at from both sides. But I just loved those women. They'd poke fun at me, and it was a hilariously good time. Plus, I was making pretty good money all the while.

The old timers who'd been in Memphis, running their businesses since the fifties and sixties, were getting ready to retire. They ran their companies by the books, and they were stern in their perspectives of the world. Then, in the eighties, they began to hire younger workers. All the young guys they hired would walk back and forth, smoking away [back then you could smoke in the office, and even go out for drinks over lunch], and sometimes would give the girls a hard time.

Down south, race is - even today - a touchy subject. And of course, any time skin color became an issue in the office, I was in the middle of it just because I was friends with all the black girls. Lucky I was, for how amazing these lifelong friendships have turned out to be! We all just had a blast working there together.

I had the honor to work for Ronald Reagan's campaign around this same time. I held both positions, working at the power company and part-time for Reagan's campaign, while also in the lifestyle. Of course, my time with Reagan ended in 1984. It was such an honor to work on that campaign. I met so many incredible people along the way. And honestly, my sexuality never really came up; it wasn't an issue.

I've got to say, while I am all for equality, in all regards, sexuality has become much too pronounced of a topic in our politics today. As I've said, I am a total history buff, and have forever held firm to the idea that our Constitution is divine. Our founding of this beautiful nation was predestined. I've read books about the men who wrote and signed the constitution, and what they had to go through to create this country. Something like ours was new; had never been done before. It was a new concept that's now lasted for almost 250 years and it is, indeed, divine.

Mormons believe that the coming forth of the Book of Mormon and the restoration of the gospel through Joseph Smith and the Latter Day Saints Church was the vehicle through which this country was organized. With freedom of religion as a given right in the USA, it was really the only place where the church could be restored; therefore, we believe the constitution is of divine origins.

I would often tell my gay friends about this, but to be honest, you often can't dig too deeply into the religious aspect with some people, and thus have to approach the ideas from a different angle. Too many individuals push religion away due to the stigmas that surround organized religions in the media. It's too bad…. Really, all the media seems to do is make things worse.

I just do not think the younger generations are igniting the priorities that are most poignant in our country. Our country and our sexuality do not need to be so intertwined as they are now. Sexuality is quite irrelevant to the world on a larger scale, and to our country; to its purpose. The problem is, things have gotten quite out of hand, in many respects, and on both sides of the struggle. The state of the world is just so foggy and clogged now. Perhaps, I just miss the simplicity, as I am now so often having to catch up, myself, to the developments in [for extreme lack of a better word] *sexual politics.*

When I was younger, I reasoned that I wanted "adults" to run the country, so that I was free enough to run around and goof off. I have always been a conservative, because that is what works the best, to me. Less taxes and smaller government is best, overall, in creating wealth that lifts people out of poverty. More spending, in order to stimulate demand, is detrimental to society, in my opinion.

Revisionist Liberal media has always tried to paint Ronald Reagan into a corner when it's come to the AIDS crisis. Many have said that he didn't spring into action with enough vigor, which is what then allowed the disease to spread. The thing is, however; he never could've known. None of us knew. Say you had promiscuous sex with the wrong person. Bam, a year later you may find yourself looking like a bag of bones, awaiting the end.

A parallel to today's world would, perhaps, be the outbreak of HPV in young women. Untraceable in men, misunderstood, easily contractible, and with varying degrees of horrible symptoms [although not quite so dramatic of a decline as compared to AIDS]. And here, nobody's blaming Obama for the steady rise of cervical cancer in women today. Reagan was one of the most amazing presidents of the modern era, and I do not feel it is just to place all blame on him. It was a tough time.

Back then, they even had an entire wing of the hospital quarantined for the handling of AIDS, alone. The disease was brutal, and had spread like wildfire before anyone even knew what was happening. I knew some great people, men and women, who died as a result of HIV. They just slept with the wrong person, and now they're gone.

What about me? Why do I get to be here? Why do I get to experience the blessings I have, throughout my life, unscathed?

The first person I knew that died from HIV was named Aubrey. He was the sweetest guy, and was the grandson of one of our neighbors growing up. He was searching in his own life and even went to a Stake Conference with me in Memphis early on. He moved to Dallas and, unwittingly, came down with the disease. I remember going to see him at the hospital. This was early on in the outbreak, and as medical care wasn't sure yet of how to treat it exactly, they had the whole end of the wing taped off with plastic, in isolation. Aubrey's parents were beside themselves, as was, especially, his brother. I served as pall-bearer in his funeral. I often think of that boy. He was definitely pure in heart… It was just bad timing, I guess.

I remember specific people who died of HIV. Vibrant, alive people, who had high hopes for their own futures… One such man was Larry: the sweetest, most gentle guy. Absolutely no guile in this guy whatsoever. A guy who slept with the wrong person, and was lost. I went to his funeral, where these guys were making crude remarks on his lifestyle: completely disrespecting the deceased due to judgement and an ignorant immaturity. It absolutely infuriated me, how they were acting. As if *they* are to judge. Really, as if any of us are to judge! Let's leave it to the Lord.

Each person who passed on from AIDS during that time changed me, and made me more determined to make changes and figure out how to get to where I wanted in this life.

I bought my first house on Carr Street at this time. I was twenty-six, and had a blast the entire time I lived there. My neighbors, friends and I partied without any sense of remorse. I was still immature in some ways; still finding my way.

My friend Jack lived across the street from the house I ended up buying, and was the one who originally encouraged me to move there. He even helped me buy my house! He wanted me to live near him and his buddies over there, and so I did, and I ended up loving my little place, especially since it was one of the only non-shotguns on the street! Every other house was no wider than twelve feet, and shaped like a trolley car; ironically enough because the workers at the turn-of-the-century rode a trolley car down the middle of that street to get to their houses.

They were known as "Shotgun Houses" because they were structured like a single barrel. A super tight fit, where you would enter through one door and then move straight through the house: through the living room to the kitchen, bathroom, bedroom, and then inevitably exit through the back door. Each room was connected, leading into the next.

A lot of gay and artsy people lived on that street, and everybody knew everybody else. You'd take a step outside your front door and immediately see other people you knew. It was a nice quaint little side street. At least, until we would have a party.

I built this beautiful pool in the back of my house, and would throw grandiose pool parties all the time while I lived there. Every year, we would have a block party with nearly 200 people in attendance, all packed into that little street. The energy was enigmatic. Between my good friends at the power plant, and my community on Carr street, I was having a grand ol' time.

People always used to bring me gifts when they came to my parties, which I always found so delightful. Often it would be a bottle of wine, or something of that sort, but there was this one gift I received that has really stuck with me over the years. Somebody brought me a tiny little music box that looked like a Baptist church, and had a cross on the top. I loved it! I guess that meant I was known as the "religious" one of the friend group, and found it to be a huge compliment. I remember twisting the little steeple on the top of the church so that it would play music.

I never minded when those queens would give me a hard time about my adoration for the church. I always took it to mean that I was just being myself: an imperfect believer. Throughout my eight years spent living on Carr street, though I had a stellar community and loved everyone I hung around, I was consistently drawn back to the church. I always craved the reverence and the scriptures. I never lost sight, nor was I ever totally out of touch with my faith. All my senses were directed upwards. And nothing could distract me from that. Not ever.

I really did feel comfortable in that whole community - the whole life I had built while living there - but I always knew my time with the gay community would end someday. I just didn't know when or how. I always felt it, in my heart, that I was an outsider in a lot of ways; as though I had this inner source of light, telling me wordlessly where I was headed and who I really was. I even used to tell people,

Someday, I'm going to get to the Temple.

It was creeping towards 1994, and I was still partying away at my humble abode, when tragedy struck. My absolute favorite aunt, Wylodine, passed away quite suddenly.

She was only sixty-two. I only got to speak with her on the phone the day before she passed, and wasn't able to go to Shreveport to actually be there with her. Unfortunately, I had a huge party scheduled for that weekend, and there was just no way of cancelling such a thing on such short notice. At least, not back then, before the social media surge.

I'd always been so close to her, as I've mentioned before, and so I took it as quite a blow to not be able to be there for her, or with her. I had always loved her so. When she passed, the words *I knew you'd tell me* echoed in my ears. I had always taken strength from what she said, and went onward in my life, better for it.

When I spoke to her on the phone before her passing, she told me that they had done a carotid ultrasound. She said, *Keith, they tell me that the inside of my veins are like peanut butter*, meaning her main veins were so clogged up with fat that they were sluggish and slow-moving. I encouraged her that everything would be fine, as she was set to have surgery the next day, but she didn't make it. She passed on the table. Oh man, was I devastated.

I was a nervous wreck that weekend, but I had all these people coming to my house for a party, so I had to reel in my emotions. Though I didn't make the funeral, I was able to be there for her burial, back up in Mississippi. Our family cemetery is on the original site of one of the first LDS churches in MS, where my grandmother and our other ancestors are buried.

Soon thereafter, one of my former roommates, Derick, found out he was HIV positive. Being the natural caretaker that I am, I wanted to do whatever I could for him. I immediately called him and said,

Look, just move back in, and you can just live here. No bills; no nothing.

But he refused, and I was so upset with him. Even back then, I wanted what I wanted: I wanted Derick to be okay, and was stubborn about it. AIDS killed back then; it was pretty much a death sentence. I said back to him, *Look, I'm offering you the opportunity to come back here, and have a place to be taken care of.* He had two kids from a previous marriage, but I was afraid he would have little support there. Still, he refused.

I know, truly, that this was my providence for getting out of Memphis, however. I absolutely had to leave. At that time, living the lifestyle that I was, there was absolutely no way I could've openly said to the community,

Alrighty, everyone, I'm gonna go date women now. You know, switch up my life a little, but I'll see you guys around!

Uh… Nu-uh. My life needed a real transition; a reinvention. I was thinking more and more about my transition at this time - that picture was becoming more and more clear to me - but I was still apprehensive, and I knew it couldn't all happen while I was still in Memphis.

I was too engrossed in the gay culture of Memphis to be able to stay there, and still allow for this reinvention. Of course, I was devastated to go: sad to leave the people, the parties, and the good friends. I didn't want to leave what was familiar, but I knew what I was heading towards. So I set a date, and started making plans to move to Dallas. I was filled with a mingling of sadness and anger at Derick's situation at the same time, however, which made the whole move taste even more bittersweet.

Otherwise, when I spoke of making these changes in my life as I matured, I had several friends of years and years tell me I was crazy, and that, if I wanted to do this, they didn't want to keep in contact.

I thought, so be it. I felt something was happening, and I was going to follow it.

CHAPTER FIVE

Dallas: 1995 – 2000

I moved from Memphis to Dallas on New Year's Day: January

1st, 1995. Derick's little brother, Jason, and his friend David, lived there at the time, so I decided to move in with the pair of them for awhile, before getting a place of my own.

When I reflect back, I just know I had divine help in getting out of Memphis. I see this especially in regard to how much the move influenced my overall choices. I was stuck in a very familiar groove back in Memphis, and wasn't ever going to get out alive, unless I made some *real* change. And as the years progressed, I knew I would have to start making a decision about my future. I knew I wanted an eternal family, but it was obvious that I had some steps yet to take before reaching such a pinnacle.

Even as I went through the relationships I had with guys, each one was a bit shorter than the last, and each became less and less serious. I never really let the relationships get past a certain point. I knew I was going to make a decision, and I knew the decision I was going to make… so what was stopping me? I'm not sure. Fear, probably. I wasn't sure how to handle a real woman, as I'd always been a bit too intimidated. I wasn't sure who would accept and love me with my past; for exactly who I truly am as an individual.

Back while I was in Memphis, I didn't quite know all this. I didn't really know what was going on at all. What I did know was that I needed to get out of Memphis in order to get myself on the right path. I needed to get going with my hopes and plans and true desires if I was going to have enough time to really appreciate them. But anyways, I wasn't quite privy to all this just yet. More like, I was just doing my thing and humbly searching.

I was gently transitioning myself into an absolute closeness with my Heavenly Father. I didn't know it at the time, but I was moving forward, past those feelings, and past my trial with same sex attraction. The projection of my underdeveloped and unloved traits faded with time, as I came to truly understand myself and the way I move through the world. I came to understand what truly mattered most to me in this life. I came to see what I most desired, and what would grant me absolute closeness with my Heavenly Father.

As I was on my way out of Memphis, I really dug into a study of the Old Testament. I bought thick books and read it all. Cleon Skousen, an author from BYU (Brigham Young University), had written a set of books in the fifties about the Old Testament. This deep study has enriched my perspectives of Israel, and all peoples in the throes of conflict and turmoil. I see how these Old Testament teachings are ever applicable, even today, and especially concerning the righteous, or those who try to receive divine help.

The rebellious do not try to contact divinity; the humble ask and pray.

That is why I am a huge supporter of Israel today. In the Old Testament, the Lord blessed the Jews, and so long as they did whatever He told them to do, they would defeat their enemies. Over and over and over, this happened. They would triumph every single time. Only when the Jews did not do as the Lord had purveyed, were they conquered by their enemies. [Every. Single. Time.]

The Lord preserved the Jews as His people, and so long as they were loyal and faithful and true to His love, He would protect them with His. **When we are devout, the Lord blesses us. But when we disobey or disregard the Lord's guidance, we fail to experience the beauty of His divinity.** It's all so evident in the Old Testament, and it's all still so relevant now. Looking back, I see that this study was helping me to move my life closer to where I wanted to be.

I *love* Texas, and Dallas is like no other place in the world. At the time, their economy was awesome, so it was a constant party. And not just in spots: the whole city was celebrating. There's a whole lot of money and pretty people living in that town, and at the time that all looked pretty good to me. I looked forward to the idea of making good money and making new friends. Though, I wasn't so much looking for the same scene I had just left behind in Memphis. Not at all.

I started working in the financial sector in customer service when I first got to Dallas, which was basically what I had done back in Memphis, working for FedEx. However, my roommates were all waiters in these fine dining restaurants and they were pulling in some pretty crazy money. Of course, as we were in Dallas, they partied it all away night after night. I wanted to make crazy money, and I wanted to party it away, too. So I got a job in a restaurant.

None of us saved our money, but one year I pulled in nearly eighty thousand dollars in cash! And on top of that, we all got to drink the most amazing wine while we worked, and hang out and get to know one another. I was especially drawn, at the time, to the female chef of the restaurant. I was trying to branch out a little more, and was attempting to get to know myself around women in a romantic sense.

I began to, after becoming accustomed to the city's rhythm, attend church again. I always felt so comfortable and happy, and even amidst so much fun and partying there in Dallas - even in the midst of all that madness - I was still drawn to study the gospels. I read quite a few Doctrinal Commentaries, to get a better understanding of the Old Testament and the Scriptures. I never felt like a hypocrite, having an attraction to men and studying the gospels simultaneously. I knew my SSA was something the Lord would help me navigate; a trial I would conquer if I wanted to get to the Temple.

After a few years, I really was over the party scene there. As much as I have always loved a good time, I was wanting something more *real*; something more serious and fulfilling. I wanted to move, but wasn't really sure what to do or where to go. I really depended on Jason quite a bit at the time, and though he was some ten years younger than myself, he was very strong and outgoing. He could naturally and effortlessly get whatever he wanted.

Unfortunately, one thing he couldn't do anything about was when David, his friend and our other roommate, got sick. Halfway through 1997, David lost his father to cancer, and about six months later his mother died suddenly from a heart attack, as well. He was an absolute emotional wreck, and his immune system started to fail as a result. It turned out that he was HIV-positive, but had never done anything about it; he never took any medication or anything. He declined rapidly, until the doctors decided to put him on hospice in January of 1999. One morning a short while later, he died in our apartment.

I remember the night we felt him going. We stayed up all night, that night, with his sister who'd come to stay with us as soon as David began to decline. His poor sister had lost her entire family in a year, and when David went, her screams of grief and agony could be heard for blocks and blocks. Her sorrow was so chilling. It was so sad to not be able to do a thing to console her.

By the mid-90s you did not see so many people die from HIV as in the mid-80s, but there it was: the still, cold reality. We lived in a three-story walk-up at the time. So when workers came to take the body away, they couldn't get the gurney up the second floor, and I had to intervene. After they wrapped his body, I literally just picked him up and carried him down the stairs. I'm telling you now: this was no problem for me. I mean, I'm pretty strong, mind you, and I could've picked him up anyway, but picking him up then was like lifting up a bag of empty aluminum cans. He was really just bones, and he was six feet tall! Which was, of course, the reason they couldn't get the gurney up there in the first place.

This event affected me very deeply. I felt more of a sense of urgency to push forward and get on with my own journey; I just didn't know exactly what to do. I know in my heart, though, that death is another step in our eternal progression. The journey doesn't end in death; it's all in God's plan for us.

After David passed, it was just Jason and I living in that apartment, both working and doing our best to move forward. Our apartment was a bit quieter now, but we tried to get through those ensuing weeks. I started back at work in the restaurant, and tried to get back into the swing of things.

One Friday night in the restaurant where I worked, I waited on a table with an angel sitting there. Her name was Jo West, and she was from the hill country: Leakey, Texas. She came to *Parigi* ["Paris" in Italian], where I was working as a waiter, and for three nights, she left me ridiculous tips.

She was in town to see a play, so the day of the performance, I went to the Melrose Hotel in Oak Lawn where she was staying. I took a five dollar bunch of gladiolus to the concierge of that hotel and had him put them in her room with a note simply saying,

Hope the play was awesome! -Keith

After that, we became fast friends and whenever she would come to Dallas, we'd go to plays and concerts galore. We went to NYC together for her birthday one year, stayed at the Waldorf, and met several famous people. She was an awesome friend - *so much fun* - and I love her very much.

She had three children I came to know quite well, who were all just slightly younger than myself. Her youngest son, Adam was an awesome guy. He met and married this beautiful LDS girl from Nevada. Soon they were married, he joined the church, and they were sealed in the Temple. This guy was one of the most pure in heart people I've ever met. Each time I saw him, he wanted to talk about what he had learned in his study, and share the awesome talks he'd heard in General Conference. Associating with people like him helped push me toward making the changes I needed to enter the Temple. I know that Adam West [*not* Batman] pushed me to my goal of the Temple.

Then, even more help arrived in my life. This nice-looking dude came in to apply for a job. He wasn't gay, but I couldn't help but be drawn to him - heck, everyone's breath in that restaurant caught the day he walked in. And he was very accepting. Absolutely everyone wanted to get in his face. He was a dark-haired surfer from South Texas, with an unbelievable physique, and an even more unbelievable personality.

Darren was his name. People often stopped dead in their tracks when he moseyed on by. And then they would speak with him, and realize what a sweet-natured personality he had. He was especially appreciated there in Dallas, as it was so superficial and all, and whenever he would bartend, people would pack all in the restaurant just to look at him - just to be around him! Well, he ended up getting hired at Parigi, of course, and - out of everyone else there - wanted to hang out with *me*.

Absolutely everyone who met Darren fawned over him, and the whole area fell in love with him instantly [albeit only for his more superficial aspects, when there was so much more there]. He was really quite spiritual, and I could tell that from the start. I never fawned over him, though, even though I thought he was great. I was a tad bit older than the other waiters in the restaurant, still growing in maturity, and on the path to figuring out what it was I *really* wanted [on the longer term as compared to instant gratification]. I was asking more of myself, and really digging in to the tougher aspects of what I wanted. I was finally asking the tough questions, as though in subconscious anticipation for my transition from men to women. I would ask myself,

*Well, why **don't** you like women? Why?? What is it that keeps you from pursuing **that** attraction; **those** desires?*

I began to realize, well, that I do like women. I really do; I always have. I just don't have any practice at it, and it's all been a bit more intimidating for me, as a result.

I mean, let's be honest here: dating women after men was going to be a whole different ball game. And the Dallas Party Scene hadn't prepared me for any of it. This old friend of mine had always dated Dallas Cowboy Cheerleaders, and he would often tell me of his escapades with the gorgeous Dallas women. But I knew I could never even touch that life! I was too intimidated. I mean, I was only just getting accustomed to women in general, and was starting to feel more vulnerable about myself in that setting, on the whole. And that Big Dallas Hair was enough by itself to intimidate a guy! But I also understood that *all that* wasn't what I even wanted in the long run, anyways, so I never really pursued it.

Even when a few women approached me over the years [a few even wanted to *have a baby*]. I was getting there, sure, but I wanted to build that sort of life with a solid LDS girl to keep me and my kids in line with the Lord! Getting together with some party girl I just met would have been the furthest thing from what I wanted.

I went to see a psychologist in Dallas, who I found through the Mormon social services, to speak with someone about making my transition to women. He said to me in one of our sessions,

*Well, do you **want** to?*

And I said, *Well, the church and all its teachings are true, right?*

Well, yeah of course, but you don't have to do this. You can be gay. It's alright.

And I understood what he meant. He was correct in every way. I didn't *have to*, and I knew I wouldn't go to hell for it or anything, but I wanted to. I wanted to find a good, strong-willed woman to have and to hold by my side, and to protect with all my might. I wanted to live up to my full potential: I wanted to get married in the Temple, and I wanted to have an eternal family. And, if I wanted these things in my life, I would have to exercise a little faith.

I would go to the bookstore all the time while living in Dallas, and buy these big books to use to study the Gospel. That was all that could really give me comfort through such a tricky time of transition and, what was, the penultimate reinvention of my sexuality and interests. I knew, always, in my heart, that I was going to be alright, and was reassuringly reminded of that whenever I studied. I bought doctrinal commentaries on the Book of Mormon, and continued to read what interested me. I plunged into aspects of the restored gospel. One by Jefferey R Holland: *Christ and the New Covenant*, and another, by Frederic W Farrar: *The Life of Christ*.

My cousin, Shannon [on my mother's side], lives in Lubbock, a small town way out in West Texas. She got married at a winery out there in 1997, so I decided to drive to partake in the ceremony and celebrations. Well, it is *not* a short drive, and even though I wasn't crossing over any state lines, it was quite the trip. I drove my big, old, long Lincoln Mark V, sitting with myself in that dry sunlight, the sun beating down on me through the open sunroof, and breeze flipping through the cabin and its leather seats. That was a good drive.

Shannon's wedding was an absolute fairytale. She was brought to the ceremony in this huge carriage, led by enormous, gorgeous Clydesdale horses. It was such a beautiful celebration. On the way back to Dallas after the celebrations were over, I noticed an African

American family standing by the side of the road. A man, a woman, and their clearly newborn baby - he couldn't have even been a year old. They were obviously hoping to find someone to give them a ride, and I just couldn't help but stop for that baby.

They got in my car after putting all of their belongings in my trunk. Though I really don't make a habit of picking up hitchhikers, my gut told me not to worry about these folks. One of their belongings was this peculiarly wrapped Styrofoam ice chest that was broken apart in places, and filled to the brim with PBR, pigskins, and other wild stuff. I thought it was odd, but didn't question.

It must have been a thousand degrees that day, and so the minute they got in, I cranked the AC and told the woman to put her baby under it to cool him off. He looked filthy, and his little diaper was simply not sufficient for their situation. As soon as the little tyke felt the cool air, though, he stopped fussing and fell asleep.

After a short while, a highway patrol officer pulled me over. He called me to the back of my car and discreetly asked me "if everything was alright". Clearly thinking I was in some sort of danger, he looked at me with worried eyes and awaited my answer. I was surprised [though I guess I shouldn't have been - me in all my pristine, gay glory, driving around a disheveled black family of three], and immediately stopped in my tracks.

What? I asked, by default. *Oh, no… everything's fine! I don't usually pick up hitchhikers, but they had this baby out here, and I'm just by myself and I didn't care, so I picked them up.*

He smirked and walked off after my response, the expression on his face revealing how he never would've done what I had. I was like, *pft, whatever*, and got back in the car without mentioning, to the family, what the cop had said [of course - I could never be so rude].

Well wouldn't you know, we didn't make it five minutes after that encounter, before the Lincoln completely overheated! There I was, out in the middle of nowhere in that crazy Texas heat, with these strangers, their baby, and a bucket of beer in the back, and now we had to pull over. I was *flipping* out inside. I had absolutely no idea what I was gonna do, and here, now, I felt responsible for these other people.

The dad then turned to me and said, *I'll take care of it.*

He got out of the car and went to the trunk to pull out one of the ice waters he'd had stored in his Styrofoam box. He then popped open the hood and poured the contents of the cold liquid over the radiator, immediately cooling the car down. I had no idea you could do that! So then I knew, that had I not picked these people up, I would have been stranded, by myself, and without any help in the crazy heat. Sitting pretty, stranded under the scorching Texas heat.

After a little bit, we were able to get back on the road, and I took them to their destination of Fort Worth. Soon after, I was back in Dallas, safe and sound, as well.

I find this to be a clear example of God's grace on Earth. I know it was his love and support that guided me through that event, and connected me with the right people to where, not only my situation was made better, but so was this whole other family's! And this is just *one* example in my life, where I've felt that I was looked after or had some semblance of divine protection. These two other times, I was driving on the interstate at a steady clip when accidents unfolded all around me, yet I remained untouched. Coincidences? Perhaps, perhaps... but I choose to believe otherwise.

Just as I choose to believe otherwise with Darren. I knew that we were placed in one another's lives for a divine reason. He was exactly the person to help me take the steps necessary to find my path, just as I was able to be there for him, and help him find his way.

He had just broken up with a long-term girlfriend before moving back to Dallas [from Florida] to be closer to his mother. We became fast friends, and I remember we used to have all these conversations about pre-Earth life, the cosmos, God, souls, divine this, and divine that. He was very spiritual, and quite detached from material desires. At times, he would even just go and hang out with homeless people. Darren was so well read, and could express himself so well: the guy had even [not only] read and understood Plato, but could colloquially quote it in careless conversation.

The more conversations we had, and the deeper we got with one another, the more I started to realize, and even told him, *Man, you sound like a Mormon. What is up with that?* We agreed on absolutely everything.

After a time, he moved in with Jason and I, and the three of us were working away, when he decided to go back to Florida. I was devastated, as he had become my best friend. I loved having him in my life. When I was with him, I was studying, and I was much more serious and focused on what really mattered. And we both had such a great time with that! It took me a few months after he left to get over his absence, and I even re-immersed myself into the Dallas Party Scene to soften the blow of his exit somewhat.

It was like walking back into the flames, and looking at the threshold with a foreboding feeling filling my face, as I braced for what could be. That Party Scene. I'm telling you, it'll kill you.

I wanted to be with someone romantically after Darren left, as I had felt so close to him and then lost him altogether. I never crushed on him or anything. Just, he was exactly the friend I needed. I was so easily able to be my best self around him. He encouraged me to branch out with my personal goals. You know, the other friends I had there were in *no way* focused enough to discuss the things we could dig into when we hung out, and I really missed that.

I tried talking to some of the girls there, and tried to find interest in those I met, but nothing really panned out. Plus, I knew that when I was to find a woman, she would be no girl at all, but instead a fierce, strong woman with an even stronger testimony. I wanted someone who could potentially help to keep me in line, and support my best self as I supported hers.

I wanted a happy marriage; a Temple Marriage, and knew that when I did find the right woman, I would be willing to do anything to be the man that she needed me to. Although I hadn't had any heavy, prospective relationships by that time, I knew and understood all that it would take to foster and create a happy home. And I wanted it. I was willing to do whatever it took to get to that point, and was starting to open my mind to the future that was beginning to turn to face me.

In line with this, I really started trying to go back to the church.

Absolutely every Sunday I would try to attend service; however, I would often get a call from the restaurant, telling me that I could make three hundred dollars if I worked the party that was coming in that afternoon. Therefore, I wouldn't go to church, and made the three hundred dollars instead. I knew this was my being pulled back, tempted away from what was good for me; forces were constantly attempting to block the pathway to what I truly wanted.

Then one weekend, Genesis - a group of Mormon gays trying to live the standards of the gospel - were having a convention in Salt Lake City, Utah. I decided to go, not because I really needed a support group for my own journey navigating my SSA and religion at the time, but really just because I had a bunch of money at the time, could travel or do whatever I wanted, and thought it'd be nice to do that around like-minded individuals. I was looking forward to making some friends who were involved in the church, instead of the Dallas Party Scene, but more than anything I was curious to hear how others' experiences compared with mine.

The conference was awesome! As always, a speaker from the Relief Society General Presidency spoke, giving encouragement to all those who try to navigate their struggles to be closer to Christ.

About a minute after I got off that plane in Salt Lake, however, I was approached by some guy who wanted to hang out. Where, once in my life, I would have felt excited by the idea of being with a man, that feeling was dissipating; barely embers in an already forgotten fire. I politely declined the guy's offer, and reckoned with the prevalent shift in my wants and desires.

I was focused, ready to move forward.

After the weekend in Salt Lake, when I arrived back to work, the phone rang. I had recently switched restaurants, working at a place different from Parigi. On the phone was Darren, of all people, back in town and wanting to see me! He just popped back up, man, and at the perfect time. Here I was, about to go meet up again with this group of Mormon gay guys; about to make some decisions about where to live and what to do next, and he just so happened to come back into my life. Just as I was feeling the crest of the wave of change, he came around and surfed us both to a new shoreline.

As we were talking on his day in town, we got to a point where I heard myself saying,

You're a surfer and a server; I'm a server as well, and we could do all that anywhere with an ocean line. Heck, why are we living here, when we could be living somewhere incredible and doing all that?

So we decided together: *We're moving to Hawaii!*

I know the Lord put Darren back in my life at the right time, to help steer me in the right direction; the best direction for me. As I had been reading the scriptures and studying the gospel all this time, I had already been building momentum around my strength and self-confidence; I had already wanted to get out of Dallas when he called. I still get emotional about it, as it was a truly life changing current for me.

At the time, there were a lot of different options for what to do next, but I wasn't sure which way to go. Jason wanted me to move to Fort Lauderdale with him, but I knew I couldn't do that: Ft. Lauderdale is a gay mecca, and that surely would have taken me further away from what I most wanted. Jason did move to Ft. Lauderdale, and is currently a real estate broker there. We keep in touch, and it's always good to hear from him.

I knew I was gonna have to do something about the changes happening inside, and here was the answer. I could've stayed in Dallas and lived the rest of my life there: partying, and having boyfriends and whatnot, but I did not want all that; I didn't want any of it.

I initially left Memphis to get away from this life of partying, but it was basically from the frying pan to the fire. I really didn't realize the party scene would be even bigger in Dallas! I knew in my heart, that what I needed most was to get away from the Dallas Party Scene, and especially so if I was going to make all the big changes I hoped to.

CHAPTER SIX

Honolulu: 2000 – 2001

I moved to Dallas in January of 1995, and was on my way out in January of 2000. I was there exactly five years. We arrived on the island with the New Year on the Millennium! And just as the century turned, so did my life flip around. Here I was, forty years old and living in Hawaii with my best friend, away from all other friends and family, and figuring it all out for myself, in a new place, all over again.

Well, we really struggled when we first moved there. It was rough. We didn't have a whole lot of money, and had a bit harder of a time than we'd thought finding work. I was always urging Darren to take part in these dance contests that were always popping up on Honolulu; he could dance like a fool, popping and locking and shaking it like nobody's business. He ended up competing in a few of the contests, and won a couple of times, which really helped our collective finances at the time.

It took me a bit, but once I did find a job, it was a really great one. My money was just about run out, when I found this job working for the Plaza Club, a private dinner club that was actually based in Dallas as ClubCorp, with locations all over the world. I was a front waiter there, and with my thick southern accent and a tuxedo, I made great money doing it. I made a commission on all the wine that was sold while I worked. It was a great place: the Filipino back waiters put on a bit of a show tossing their tableside Caesar salads, and igniting their flambéed bananas foster and cherries jubilee for the guests.

Darren taught me how to longboard and surf that winter we moved. He had always been so active in that way; so talented at longboarding and surfing. And so, at forty years old, there I was, learning how to longboard and skateboard and surf. I skate and longboard all over the place now, happy to have the skills. When Darren taught me how to surf, I would just marvel at his abilities, and try to catch on quickly.

In January of 2000, I found myself surfing North Shore Oahu with waves like three-story buildings crashing over one another. I could have easily died, and had absolutely no business being out there. Darren, as excellent a surfer as he was, wasn't even able to enjoy himself as he spent all his extra energy on keeping me alive; making sure that I was paying the adequate amount of attention to the next set of waves rolling in.

I decided when we got to Hawaii that I was going to go to school and become a nurse. I knew my plan. I have six first cousins who are all nurses, and I knew if I were to marry, I would want a profession where I would always have a job, no matter the economy or location.

Once Darren and I settled into Honolulu a bit more, I started back at church, and it was awesome. Lei's and *Aloha* every Sunday at Church. My ward was located in the Honolulu Tabernacle, which was built back in the 1940's on Beretania Avenue. A short time after arriving in Hawaii, I heard through church that President Hinckley was holding a fireside talk at BYU-Hawaii, as he was visiting the islands to dedicate the new Temple on Big Island. I took the bus out to Laie and noticed the diversity of the church in the islands along my way. That was so awesome, and I felt that the Lord kept leading me to places that would be of significance to me in my new life.

There are, somewhat surprisingly to most people, lots of Mormons in the South Pacific. And whenever you go to church in Honolulu, you might see people from across the globe, as it is such an epicenter of its own.

All in all, I was just thrilled with the island life!

I started thinking that I would just stay in Hawaii and live there forever. I thought, maybe, I would find a nice local girl, and never go back to the south again! But, it wasn't meant to be. I went to all the singles functions on that island, especially frequenting all functions for the *five* different stakes on the island. Each stake there had about seven wards. This meant that there were girls everywhere, and so many that should've been prospects for me. I felt I was reasonably attractive, and so were many of them, but it just didn't happen. I just didn't feel it. And for those two years I spent completing my prerequisites for nursing, I still hadn't met anyone - not in all that time. I mean, I made plenty of friends at church, and it was great, but I was searching for more.

I never had even one minute of island fever, the whole time I lived in Hawaii. I loved it there, and still do.

One day, I met a couple on the beach. They were from Sydney, Australia, and ended up hosting me for a week down under. At the time, I was between jobs, so travelling there served as a fabulous distraction. They had a sailboat, and took me out on the water around the famous opera house in the harbor. We partied at this huge dance club in downtown Sydney, and I just had an amazing time there, overall.

When I came back from that trip, I found that Darren had started to go to church with some students from the University of Hawaii. It was one of those evangelical youth churches with services held in an auditorium, where they would turn flips for Jesus as part of their praise. Darren had wanted me to go with him, but I really didn't want to miss out on my own ward. I did decide to go with him eventually, as I really wanted to support and encourage him to do what made him feel good. I had never been one to preach to him or any of that, but just wanted to support whatever it was he wanted spiritually.

There was a stage down there in the auditorium, and all the young college kids would line up, take a running start from one end of the stage, and then Cartwheel for Jesus! I thought it was really different for him. It was surely different than what I was accustomed to, but I was happy for him to go. On the way out of that auditorium stood this big tub of water. The kids would get into the water and get baptized real quick on their way home after service. Very different from the structured Mormon Sacrament meeting, but I was really happy he was going.

So then, after I went to his church, he decided to come to the ward with me. Mormon services are much more reverent in nature, and he got quite emotional as the meeting progressed. I looked over there at him during the sacrament, the Lord's supper, and he was just in tears. He really didn't say much the rest of the day, and then school resumed on Monday as the week began.

The following Thursday, there was a knock on the door. I answered, and there stood two sister missionaries. I thought they were just stopping by, but they said that they had an appointment with Darren. I was like, *What?* So shocked. Without telling me, Darren had made an appointment with the missionaries. And of course, being only human, they loved teaching him, especially since he was so fun to be around, and spiritual by nature. But I was so surprised. I mean, he'd said nothing!

They usually encourage friends to sit with the investigator in discussions like these, so they can help answer questions, should they decide they want to join the church. So I went into Darren's meeting with these girls. In the discussion, they usually read and teach the individual some things, while otherwise relying on the Holy Spirit to confirm what they're saying. The discussions usually last several weeks, and with each discussion, Darren came closer and closer to baptism.

Indeed, at the end of the discussions, he accepted the invitation to be baptized and I am here to tell you that there was such a strong confirmation he was doing the right thing, I could hardly contain myself. If you really want to find out whether the Book of Mormon is true, and therefore if the LDS church is the Lord's organization on the earth, you only needed to be sitting in on this meeting. Don't *even* get me started.

I knew right then and there that his baptism was not only for him and his family, but that his baptism was for *me.*

I knew it instantly. He came home from school late one night and I asked him if he'd had a late class. He said he'd gone walking past a convenience store and heard two homeless people talking about Joseph Smith, so he stopped and talked to them. I said, *brother, I have no doubt.* He was something else, I am telling you.

So, there we were in Honolulu, going to church together and trying to be good boys. I mean, we both had stopped drinking. I was trying to find a wife, and focus on what I wanted. In line with this focus, I went to see the Bishop [Bishop Chu].

I felt I was ready to go to the Temple. Any individual who wants to make commitments like these must be interviewed by both the Bishop and the Stake President. In the interview, generally the questions cover whether you believe, are willing, sustain the leaders of the church, pay a full tithe, disagree with all groups of people that fight against the church, and so on. Well, I could answer a resounding *Yes!* to each one, because I was ready to go and to wear the Temple garment. Funny though, Bishop Chu never said a thing about my Liza Minelli CD collection…. But truly, I knew if I was ready to commit, that my past actions were irrelevant.

Bishop Chu had a big impact on me. He seemed to be very stern: no nonsense; all business, but he was very understanding. Let me just say that the office of Bishop is not an easy role. Think of the people in the geographical boundaries of a Ward, which in Utah could consist of a few city blocks, and in Mississippi would consist of a few counties…. All as lay ministry without pay.

I had worried initially, in going to see him, that I would have to be formally sanctioned for my SSA. It didn't matter, really, knowing the bottom line, but I just wasn't sure, so he confirmed quickly that I wouldn't. He said,

No, no you won't, but would you like counseling?

I said in response, *No, I don't need any counseling right now. What I need is a good woman.*

I did proceed to tell him a little bit about my history, and what my goals were, and how I now needed a woman. I told him,

I'm gonna find one, and there's no way I'm going back to Mississippi, no matter what.

He was such a great help to me; his confirmation and support of my goals encouraged me as I moved forward, on the pathway to finding the future I desired.

CHAPTER SEVEN

Temple Marriage and Children: 2002 – 2010

As I continued to search for a wife; my future partner in Temple

marriage, I joined LDSsingles.com on a friend's recommendation. Online dating was in its infancy, but I decided to try it. I wasn't having much luck in finding anyone on the island, though I was always open to it, searching for any sign of connection.

Since I was living in the Pacific, whenever I would get home from a day's work, it was the middle of the night on the mainland, and I'd come home to find thirty or forty girls who had written to me on the website that day. I was astounded, honestly, by how many responses I received.

I thought, *Alrighty... Here we go... So, what would I want in a wife?*

After thinking about it, I decided that I would look for a girl that loved Primary (the children's organization). I concluded that if she loved the children, she probably understood the gospel, and would be a good mother to our kids, should we ever have any.

The profiles I sorted through were all varying degrees of women: some had children, others were divorced, some single, and what have you. These qualifiers really, quite honestly, didn't deter me. I did not care, nor dare to judge any of these women in any way. I was merely looking for my wife. And as I did, one by one, I weeded through these women's responses.

I knew in my heart, really, who I was looking for the entire time: I was looking for Brenda.

She comes from a long line of pioneers, much like me. Brenda's ancestors actually made the handcart trip across the country after Brigham Young! Her ancestors, the Eyre's, consisted of parents and two sons. They left England by ship, and after arriving in America, travelled halfway across the country, to Nauvoo, where the mother died. The father and sons then continued across the plains to Wyoming. Upon their arrival there, the father died, and the two sons continued on to the Salt Lake Valley. One of the surviving sons helped settle a small town in southern Utah. Brenda was raised in Murray, Utah, and had barely ever left the state when we met. Since then, I have dragged her hither and yon! She was quite shy at first, but over the years she has really blossomed into a more outgoing person.

I'd always known that I wanted a partner who would keep me in line. You know, they say you should marry someone you are afraid of [Kidding!]. But really, I wanted to find someone who could encourage me to be my best, and bring their best to the commitment as well. I wanted to find someone who could be a Godly mother to our children, and encourage them the same way she would me. Someone who would base our relationship on the Temple, and the future, and not so much our pasts.

Well, that's precisely Brenda. Now, whether I wanted these things in a woman because they are who Brenda is, or I wanted Brenda because she was the embodiment of these things, is another chicken or the egg sort of scenario. And really, it doesn't matter. Either way, we found one another.

After Brenda and I decided to meet in person, we had to tackle the challenge of our distance. Luckily, I often traveled for General Conference, which was held in Salt Lake City, Utah, where Brenda was living at the time. I was only able to make it work to travel her way a few times while we were [basically] long distance, but each time we got together, it was a real joy.

I thought she was beautiful from the first moment I saw her. I mean, her photo on the dating site was beautiful too, but finally seeing her face sunk a heavy truth somewhere deep inside of me. I was open from the beginning with Brenda, about my past life.

All she said was, *Alright, just don't do it anymore.*

And so I said, *I won't.*

There was no worry in my heart or head that I ever would again. I knew what I wanted now, and that was a future with her. We determined to focus our marriage on the Temple and the future, and not so much what we had been doing before. But then, that really was the last we'd spoken about it all until now. Now, I'm really baring my soul to her through this book, and through the whole process of revisiting my past, and self-analyzing my personal journey.

Anyways, we got serious pretty quickly, though I still had some schooling to finish up in Hawaii. Darren and Brenda met during that time, and he helped me pick out the ring I would take to Salt

Lake City to propose. Money was tight at the time, so I could only afford a .20 carat diamond in that ring, but we found the most beautiful one we could! He had a girlfriend on the island at that point, but since he left Honolulu to get married, we've lost touch. I'd bet my money he's still riding those waves somewhere, though, and I wouldn't be surprised if he was still in Hawaii!

I lived on the island for a total of six years before deciding to finish up my core nursing classes in Memphis, as reasons: both to be closer to Brenda, and to be around my family once more. From that point, it was easy for Brenda to come and visit me, and after a short time, we decided that she would move my way, to live in Memphis with me after we married. So after I completed my first semester of nursing school, I went to Salt Lake City, where Brenda and I were married, and then we drove cross country together to live in Mississippi while I finished school.

We got married in December of 2002, and boy was I as nervous as a cat. I was terrified, as I was supposed to be with a woman - and not just any woman, but my eternal partner! Anyways, everything worked out like gangbusters in that department, and we got on famously in every way from that point onwards. For ten years, nothing but bliss surrounded our bond. It was beautiful, and truly sacrimonious.

It felt so good to hold her, and know that we were on the path I had always dreamt of. We were both so happy to be making a new life together; starting a new adventure. She was so petite and pretty, and I was amazed at how my life had turned out since deciding to move to Hawaii.

I know in my heart that Brenda was saved for me, and that my Temple marriage to her came as a blessing from God for being patient and waiting on what He had in store for me. I never let myself become bitter, never shook my fist to Heaven for who I am, and remained open to receive His blessings.

I don't have all the answers, but what I do know in my heart to be true - what I feel to be right and true and just - I couldn't fathom letting go of or denying.

Brenda and I lived in Mississippi for two years following our wedding ceremony. Living outside Salt Lake City was a huge adjustment for Brenda. Her whole life, she'd had her own family so close, and knew what she knew. Now, I was taking her outside her element, which challenged what she knew about herself in the world. She only grew stronger because of this transitional time, and was soon the absolute embodiment of that outgoing, strong *Molly Mormon* companion I had always dreamt of. She canned vegetables, made homemade jams, and could cook these delicious dinners with ingredients and talent comparable to the five-star restaurants I'd worked at in Dallas.

I often would pinch myself, for how happy I was with Brenda. So often my mind would be consumed by the thought, *You are **really** doing it!* And I was. We were, together: Brenda and I.

The day I graduated from nursing school in December of 2004, we drove to the west coast, shipped our car across the sea, and bam! We moved back to Hawaii. Brenda had never lived in Hawaii, and as I had always loved it, I wanted her to experience and come to know and love it as well as I did!

We were trying to conceive at this point, but it just wasn't happening. Brenda was thirty-seven years old at the time and, as well, had endometriosis, which proves enough of a challenge in itself. I was forty-one at the time as well, so who knew how well my swimmers were holding up at this point. We didn't stop trying, though, and kept the faith that our children would find their way to us when they were meant to.

We didn't have a lot of money at the time, so another piece of our pull towards the island was that a single trial of In Vitro was covered by the state insurance companies in Hawaii. I guess you could say it was the straw that broke the coconut's back, and pointed our collective compass in the direction of the island.

I took my nursing boards in Hawaii [and passed!], and while waiting for my nursing license to arrive in the mail, I worked as a nurse's aide. I walked to the downtown Honolulu Post Office every day, awaiting that letter. Especially since my salary would more than double, once I had it! The sweet, local lady who saw me sitting there each day would say,

I'm sorry. No mail yet!

Finally, one day when I walked in, she spotted me in the doorway and walked toward me with an envelope in her hand. She stopped just short of me, extended her hand, and said,

Let me be the first to congratulate you, with your license as a registered nurse.

I burst into tears, right then and there, knowing that I could finally afford to support my wife and our hopes for a family.

Hereafter, I began working as a nurse in the prison system there in Hawaii, since they were paying forty dollars an hour.

After being a broke student for so long, the money was a welcome relief. Life on the Island, as I'm sure you're aware, is not cheap. And so, we had a one-bedroom apartment near Waikiki that cost us six hundred dollars a month. It wasn't anything fancy, but it's linoleum floors supported us just fine. It was in a safe area, and really, what more could you want, anyway? You're in Hawaii. We sure were thrilled with the place. We went out to dinner as often as we could afford, visited the beach, and had a great time living there for a few years.

We even had the honor of witnessing Gladys Knight do a fireside at BYU-Hawaii while we lived there! She joined the Mormon church in the late nineties, and her kids were raised Mormon, as well. She came to BYU-Hawaii to celebrate the 50th Jubilee in 2005, as well as share the story of how she found the church! Plus, while she was there, she performed a Motown show. So Brenda and I drove to the other side of Oahu for the weekend to be a part of it all, and what a treat that was! She is a special woman, that's for sure!

Our In Vitro trial in 2006 was unsuccessful, so we began to widen our scope.

We were teaching primary school classes on Sundays at the time, which began to get our parenting wheels turning. Those adorable little kids! And as we were living in Hawaii, the children in that class were from so many diverse cultures: some were Native Islanders, Koreans, Chinese, Marshall Islanders, and Caucasians. A rainbow of beautiful children. Once we decided that adoption was our next best option, we found an agency that helped people adopt Marshall Islanders [Marshall Island is part of Micronesia]. So, we *jumped* on it.

Once we decided not to try again with the In Vitro, and instead adopt, we really felt good about the decision. Our calling in the ward was to teach primary, and seeing those adorable little kids each week sparked the inspiration within us to adopt. We knew we could love any child as our own.

The baby was to be born in Utah, as the agency was stationed in Utah, and just as well, Brenda was from Utah, so guess where we moved to next? Utah! In the summer of 2006, we abandoned the island and headed back to our amber waves of grain.

The pregnant Marshallese woman whom the agency had matched us with was unable to keep this baby as it was her third, and their family was in the midst of financial crisis. They had kept their first baby as part of their forever family, but had to adopt out her second and third pregnancies, due to a lack of resources. Their second baby [named Derek] was adopted by another family living out far west in Utah: The Greens.

When the Marshallese woman had become pregnant for a third time, she initially called the Greens to see if they wanted to adopt her other child, so that the two children could be together. Sister Green replied that she knew in her heart that their third baby was not meant to be hers, which was how we were, then, next in line. We now carry on a very solid friendship with the Green family, and our son Ethan is able to grow up knowing and hanging around his biological brother whenever possible.

Soon after we got to Utah, I started work at Salt Lake Regional Hospital. I really enjoyed my time there, and as I was an expecting [adoptive] father, the staff threw a party for me that made it all feel real. Brenda and I were so thrilled about our coming baby! It was all new for the both of us: neither one of us had ever been married, nor had any children. We spent those six months - we didn't even get the usual nine to prepare - hurriedly remodeling Brenda's rental [that she still owned from before we were married], and working like crazy to get everything ready! And very well, within six months of our arrival in Utah, we had a brand new baby.

Brenda and I were lucky enough to be in the room when our son was born. Up until the due date, we took the birth mother to her appointments, and then, on October the eleventh, out came our little, bouncing, brown baby boy! It was the most exciting thing ever. We decided to name him Ethan. Man, it was so unbelievable. He was so cute, and just screamed his head off from moment one.

We are still in connection with his true birth parents and their first child, Ethan's big sister. We see no reason to deny him these relationships with his biological family members. We are an eternal family, so as he grows older, then, he can define and form the kind of relationships with them that he so chooses.

It was very hard for the birth mother to sign the papers, however. She sat on the floor, wailing and wrestling with her decision, until she ultimately signed. It was so hard for us to watch. And who were we to say what was meant to be? So we waited, and tried to soothe her without any agenda. She was right with her decision, in the end, and I believe that we are all luckier for it, as all three siblings still visit with one another often, Ethan is not estranged in any way from contact with his biological parents, and all three children get to lead beautifully balanced lives.

We were so ecstatic to take our little Ethan in our arms, and welcome him into our eternal family. Even though Ethan is adopted, and is openly aware of the fact, we teach him of the eternal love that binds us as a forever family living under the gaze of God's love. We instill in him that our love is what makes us his parents. We are honestly raising a missionary: he already has developed a great appreciation for the sacrifices his birth mom made in allowing us to adopt and raise him.

The first thing I did after Ethan was born - besides hold him and stare at his perfect face - was go to the telephone and call home to Mississippi, to tell my family the joyous news. A close family friend, Tiffany, answered the phone [who is one to be remembered for later on in my story] and passed me around as I shared my excitement! As soon as I found my own forever family, all I wanted to do was get back home to Mississippi. I wanted my kids to grow up around my family; their family, so they could grow up around where I did, and get to know their whole, big extended family.

The entire time I was growing up, I never felt even one bit of angst, prejudice, or disrespect from my family or friends about who I was. I came from a long line of Mormons who knew that I knew the truth: that my sexuality was but a trial for me to overcome. I wanted my children to have that same system of support. As I had grown up, they always told me that they knew I would do the right thing because of my testimony, and that they knew I would try to get my life in line with the church's teachings eventually.

His first year, Ethan was colicky and horrible, screaming his head off without end. Thus, it took us about a year to get ourselves together enough to move back to Mississippi, like I wanted. We spent many a sleepless night in the recliner that year, with Ethan swaddled up and wedged under one of our arms. Even though it was a mess, it was the best thing ever. I was too terrified to even take him out of the house back then, as I was worried he would catch something. I didn't want any germs on him. Not on my baby boy.

We rented out the house in Salt Lake, and bought a house in Hernando, Mississippi. I started working for one of the local hospitals there, and we started to settle into the same ward that I had grown up in. *My* old ward.

After about a year, we moved to Senatobia, into the neighborhood of my aunt, uncle and cousins. My father's next-to-youngest sister (my aunt), her three children, and all of their families were living in this neighborhood at the time. So that's where we moved. It was a very small town, located within the ward. We really took root there for a good while.

After the housing market crashed, I decided that I wanted to go to law school, as an attempt to bring in more money. Brenda has always supported me in whatever I choose to do with my education to better our family. I decided, then, to take the LSAT a few times in Mississippi. Though I didn't do very well, I had a connection with UNLV Law School, and so I thought it may still be an option for me. Thus, I took up a nursing contract in Las Vegas for the winter of 2009, when Ethan was about three, and we moved there so I could give law school a shot. We didn't really like it there, and law school never really panned out, but we stayed through the winter before going back to Mississippi in the spring.

Ethan was about four when we decided to adopt again. We decided, this time, to apply through the church, as the agency that we had used to adopt Ethan had gone out of business. We really weren't too particular concerning the race or sex of our baby this time around. At least not originally. Unfortunately, the nearest LDS social services office was all the way in New Orleans, so, we drove all the way there to submit our paperwork, paid the thousand-dollar fee that was requested, and quickly got the ball rolling.

In the meantime, Brenda's sister in Utah was introduced to some people who knew an attorney in Phoenix; a guy who had served his LDS mission in the Marshall Islands and, after coming back to the US and going to law school, now handled domestic adoptions for Marshallese people who were already living in the US. A big plus was that it was considered a domestic adoption, as the Marshall Islands are part of the United States, like Puerto Rico, where citizens can come and go as they please without a passport or green card. [This was established due to atomic testing that had gone on during WWII on Bikini Island.]

We figured that this was the way to go, as both of our children would then be from the same island. Soon after applying, we were matched with a family, and thereafter closed our application with the LDS social services office in New Orleans.

Well, we came to find out that there was a whole community of Marshallese people relocating to Arkansas (right next to my homeland of Mississippi) to work in the chicken processing plants. They were easily able to get jobs there, even though the working conditions were not the best. So even though our attorney was in Phoenix, we were nearer to where the large community of Marshallese families were: not even five hours away from where we were living! We figured this meant that it was meant to be.

Brenda had always wanted a girl. We already had a boy, now, in Ethan, so we decided to change our sexual preference with the agency. As we already had a baby, we were chosen by a birth family in Arkansas very quickly. This pregnancy would have become the woman's ninth child, so the couple decided that they couldn't take care of any more babies. This made us breathe collectively - Brenda and I - a deep sigh of relief. It had been so difficult to watch the first time, when the birth mother wrestled with her decision as she was signing the papers in the hospital.

Soon after we were selected, the attorney called, mentioning that the family may possibly want to adopt their one-year-old to us as well, since they were so destitute, and had recognized us as dependable and loving parents. We of course agreed to take them both in, lovingly. But then, the very next day, he gave me another call, this time to inform us that they had decided not to adopt out their one-year old girl, but also that she was carrying a boy.

I told Brenda, *It's a boy, so… we're gonna have two boys.*

She just shook her head sadly, saying, *No, no…. I want to wait for another family.*

I replied back to her, *No. I don't think that's right. When you have a baby, you don't get to choose, and you get what the Heavenly Father gives you…. We will have to pray about this.*

I whispered this all to her while the attorney was still on the phone. He sensed the tension, saying, *Well… I-I'll call you back tomorrow.* And so I said, *Okay, I'll let you know….*

As soon as I hung up, I said to Brenda, *You'd better pray about this, because I don't feel good about it; you know this is our baby.*

She softly said, *Okay,* as she nodded her head, and I carried on, saying, *You don't get to choose what the Lord gives you when you're pregnant.*

The next morning, when we woke up, Brenda turned to me and said, *Ok. It is our baby. We will have two boys.*

I was happy that she had come to her own conclusions about it. *And* I was off the hook! We were, once more, on the same page, and of one heart, ready to welcome another beautiful baby into our eternal family. So I called the attorney that morning, and told him that we wanted the baby; we wanted the boy.

The baby was due about eight weeks later, which seemed to us to be quite a while, though of course it was still so much sooner than having a nine-month-long pregnancy. We prepared for his arrival, in the meantime, by buying boys clothes, toys, and tools: we bought everything. We were ready. Ready for this little one to come into our lives!

About a month before the baby's due date, the phone rang, and the attorney's rep was on the other line, this time saying,

I hope you're sitting down. It is a girl.

Well, I was floored. Neither of us could believe it! As it turned out, the birth mother had never gotten the ultrasound. She had already been pregnant eight times, so she just presumed that she knew what it was. The rep continued, with,

I'm telling you this: had you passed this baby up, I never would've told you that it was actually a girl, because I just wouldn't have wanted to break your hearts.

So there we were. Another miracle. These are *my* kids. Our kids, eternally. They were meant to be. And my life has really just, you know, been like that. All the time. I've always come out on top, after every trial or time of hardship. I'm strong, and the Lord has always been there to support and remind me of that.

Well, here we had to book it to Arkansas, as we needed to get not only our baby, but all the clothes and toys for a girl, now! Our little girl was early, and it was a five hour drive. And, *girl*, that sure was one *long* five hour drive. We could not *wait* to meet her!

As we had thought the baby was going to be a boy, we didn't have any appropriate names picked out or anything. We weren't ready! On the drive there, we drove at a breakneck speed while calling people to help us decide on a name. We were so underprepared for her arrival, but she was just a miracle. The sweetest thing; a little brown baby all bundled up, and so beautiful. We could hardly believe our lives!

We were so excited to get her back home. Ultimately, we decided to name her Ilana. It was a bit of a struggle at first, as I had really wanted to name her after my grandmother Irene, and Brenda wouldn't hear of it. Obviously, though, I wanted what I wanted, our little girl was meant to have her own, significant, meaningful name.

We brought her back home to Mississippi, and there was a big welcome sign in the living room from all my family. This big ol' banner that was draped across the front of the hall said,

Welcome to our family.

I was so thrilled to be at home with my extended family all there, and now with the fullness of my eternal family, that I never had any doubts about the decision to live and raise my kids there in Mississippi with them all.

Not at that time, at least.

CHAPTER EIGHT

The Surgery: 2011 – 2015

After we settled into Mississippi a bit more, I got a job as a

hospice nurse. I was working weekends at the hospital, which proved to be quite lucrative itself, and then during the week, I would drive around northern MS to visit patients in their homes. I loved having the freedom to move around during the week and get to know all these sweet families that were saying goodbye to their loved ones. I loved being able to help souls pass peacefully to the afterlife. On top of all that, our work group Aseracare was phenomenal, and there was this sense of family amongst the staff.

Four months after Ilana was born, Brenda was set to go into the hospital for a routine outpatient surgery. She has struggled with endometriosis her entire life, experiencing all the pains and worries that accompany such a disorder. When a woman struggles with endometriosis, they come to befriend painful symptoms, brought on by the growth of tissue on the outside of the uterus, when it should only ever be growing on the inside.

The tissues that are normally stripped away by a woman's menstrual cycle have no way of exiting the body, which forces many women into surgeries that remove these excess tissues [as well as any scar tissues or fibroids that form]. The growth of such tissue can, in itself, be very painful, as can the surgeries that are necessary to remove them.

Brenda was all set to have a laparoscopy performed by the same gynecologist she had been seeing for over three years since arriving back in Mississippi. She hadn't needed any surgeries for ten years previous to this, which was around the time when we got married. In a laparoscopy, the doctor will make a small incision and go in through the navel to lance off any fibroids that have developed in the abdomen, as well as outside and around the uterus.

What was supposed to be a one-day, outpatient surgery turned out to be a nightmare.

I took Brenda to the hospital on that Wednesday afternoon in February, ran some errands, and then headed back to get her. When I got back, ready to pick Brenda up and take her home, the doctor stopped me in the hall, saying:

I perforated her bladder, so we had to go back in, and make another incision, in order to close up that hole. We need to keep her bladder empty tonight, and she will have a Foley and stay overnight here at the hospital while we pump her full of antibiotics.

The worst form of endometriosis is when the tissue growth begins to locate itself around other vital organs. Apparently, some of Brenda's fibroids had grown all the way to her bladder, and in an attempt to remove them, the doctor accidentally nicked her bladder and made a perforation. Then, this caused an infection, which is why they decided to keep her overnight and give her the antibiotics. Keeping her overnight saved her life.

I later came to find out that Brenda's temperature had skyrocketed to 104 degrees at four am that night in the hospital, and it turned out that there were actually *five separate perforations* in her colon and bladder. Her bowel contents were leaking into her abdominal cavity, and the antibiotics were trying to take care of the infection as fast as they could, but she was continuously being poisoned by her own waste product.

An infection due to contamination like this is commonly known as sepsis, and it can easily be deadly. And the antibiotics really weren't doing her any good; especially not near enough good to fight something like sepsis!

Sepsis kills more people than heart disease and breast cancer combined. Brenda has since joined a support group, Sepsis Alliance (www.sepsisalliance.com), and has found out just how devastating and common septic shock is!

Well anyways, my whole family rallied around me, as they knew just as well as I did that something wasn't right. Everybody came up to Memphis on Saturday and said,

Get her out of here. There's something seriously wrong.

I was at that hospital day and night with Brenda, as I sure didn't trust what the hospital was doing at this point, and by Sunday, she was nearly on her deathbed. Five days, from an outpatient surgery to harboring on the brink of death. She got sicker and sicker each day. After my family arrived on Saturday, we started demanding that she be moved to the big Baptist hospital next door. So, they transferred her care over to a surgeon at the Baptist Hospital on Sunday night, and we all caravanned over there to support her and fight for her in every way we could imagine.

Had she gone right home after that initial surgery, we never would've realized what was wrong with her in enough time to save her life. A whole-bodied septic infection like that is so deadly. If we were lucky of *anything*, it was that the doctor had decided to keep her overnight after the surgery.

On Monday, the surgeon at the Baptist hospital decided to open her up, and they found her absolutely covered in feces on the inside. It was obvious that she had been leaking her bowel contents into her abdomen all weekend, and though she had been on antibiotics, nothing was done - that whole time - to try to inhibit the leakage. Though the antibiotics helped to get her this far, they had been doing nothing about the perforations or the excrement leakage. While the doctor had Brenda on the table, he had to remove almost a foot of her colon - where all the perforations were - in order to save her life. Well, Brenda came rolling down the hall in the hospital bed after what was about a six hour surgery, and all the doctor said to me was,

It was grim.

I couldn't believe it. I couldn't believe that I had almost lost Brenda like that.

In my much sought after role of a husband and father, I hadn't taken a single minute for granted since I met Brenda. As a nurse, I see this type of illness, and interact with it from time to time, but it's so much different when it's happening to someone you love: especially Your Someone.

I was numb. I was broken-hearted. But then again, I was the one walking around; Brenda was the one on a ventilator.

That doctor really did save her life. But even though he saved her life like that, and was able to repair all the damage that had been done on the inside, her stomach was still so swollen that they were not going to be able to close up her muscles for at least eighteen months.

We had tons of family and close friends waiting there, and finally we could, all of us, take a rest. Our home teachers, Brother and Sister Norris, were there all day with me.

When I first saw Brenda, she was on the ventilator, barely alive.

Each minute from here on out would be a fight. She wasn't going to be able to have solid food in her stomach for at least eight months, she was going to have PICC lines and IV nutrition running all day, and really it was all just looking so awful for her. She still had such a long road ahead of her, before she was anywhere near making a full recovery.

When I went into the room to visit with Brenda after her surgery, she was lying on the hospital bed with a ventilator running and her abdomen open to air - a six-inch hole in her freaking abdomen. There was a tube in every hole, and she was on major drips to keep her alive and sedated. It looked grim, and I thought,

Oh my gosh.

My heart was sinking; my Brenda was in so much pain! I thought,

*Oh my goodness, my babies... they need a mom, not me trying to bake cookies for them! And my Brenda! My babies need their mother... and Brenda needs to be here to **be** their mother! And I can't be without her.... What would I **do?!***

After a few days, I brought the kids there to see her, and we were looking at her, and I just couldn't believe it. Here I sat with these babies, explaining to them why their mom was unresponsive, trying to encourage their hope while also urging forth my own, and the doctors were just *not* encouraging. They'd said, *It's gonna be tough,* as each one threw me a grim, worrying look.

They didn't think she would make it, and even the nurse inside me had his doubts. But as Brenda's husband, I *knew*, without a shadow of a doubt, that she would make it fine. All simply because I knew our marriage was no accident. I was confident that, somehow, things would work out.

While Brenda stayed in the hospital, I was focused on keeping the kids' lives as normal as possible, making sure they got to primary and preschool, their Sacrament meetings, and to see Mommy whenever possible.

She came home about six months after her surgeries, after being in rehab for about four of those months. She'd basically had to learn how to walk again. And those first two months after she came home, when she was still recovering… man. She arrived weak as a kitten. She came home just a mess, and here I was the only one who could piece her back together.

Graciously, our ward rallied around me. My deep freezer was full of food. People came over to help me with the kids, so I could go to work. They even gave me gas money when I refused. She was on the prayer list around the community of every Baptist, Methodist and holy rolling church in Tate County, for which I am absolutely convinced had an influence in her recovery.

After Brenda got home, it was another four months before she could eat solid foods again. I had to work as a nurse at the hospital all day, and then come home and be a full-time nurse to my darling wife all night.

I created a system the best I could. I had PICC line dressing changes, had to track and switch out Brenda's TPN - IV nutrition, helped her go to the bathroom, and helped her move about regularly to combat any atrophy. Then, on the other end, I had to take care of the babies. This meant diapers and bottles, taking Ethan to daycare, cooking meals that satisfied each mouth independently, and parenting two children with barely the adequate energy of one.

What's more, there were the basics like laundry, lawn care, maintaining the garden, and getting some sleep to keep doing it all... I was losing my mind. And to top it off, I wasn't able to work as much as I had used to, as I needed to be there with Brenda, and for my kids, so finances were tighter than ever. I was trying, quite aggressively, to pay off this $800 second mortgage, so that I could try to have just a little bit of breathing room through it all.

I was killing myself to try to do it all. And I was scared to death, no doubt! But I'm telling you, I take care of my family.

That was my only priority, and everything I did was engineered towards this priority. At the time, I kept thinking about Joseph Smith. If he saw what he said he saw, then everything else is absolutely elementary and must be true as well. This resonance with the truth of living helped me see clearly what my purpose was.

I'm a bit of a bottom-line man, y'all, and when Brenda was sick, I was focused on *my* bottom line the whole time: to keep the family together, and keep Brenda close to the daughter she had always wanted.

I absolutely refused to let anyone else take care of my wife or my babies. I wanted my babies in the bed with me, as we prepared for mommy to come home. And then, after she was back, though I didn't want them worrying about her, I wanted them with her; with me: our eternal family all together, as it was meant.

Every so often, I would have my kids spend the night at a family or friend's place, but only when I had to work the night shift. And even then, the next morning after my shift - bright and early - I was there to get them. They're my family, and it was up to me to hold them together through this trying time.

While Brenda tried to concentrate on getting stronger, I literally did not have even one minute of peace for nearly two years. It was a constant uphill climb; a daily battle and juggling act all in one. The only peace I found was - *maybe* - when I was asleep. I just had to keep moving. I didn't complain about it; didn't pass it on for anyone else to do. I even set up sufficient help with those I trusted as a means of relieving some of my chaos, but I was in pain: it hit me financially, emotionally, and completely imploded any and all knowledge I had of time-management - I was exhausted. The only thing that got me through was that I had my family all there with me. I just had to focus, put my head down, and keep plugging away until we were out of the storm.

Now, I could figure out how to sew, cook, figure out how to raise a daughter, and figure out how to do all the things Brenda had done as a mother, but I couldn't take the place of a mother; of Brenda. And my brand new baby girl needed a mother, even more than she needed a daddy.

I needed that for her, my sweet Ilana, just as I needed it for myself. Even though I knew, as we had formed an eternal family, we would always be together in eternity, I just couldn't believe that the Heavenly Father would take Brenda - so soon - from the daughter she had always wanted. Especially before she had a chance to really *become* the mother, to her daughter, that she had always wanted to be. I was sure that the Lord would be merciful, and held that tight to my chest in hope as she was healing.

When Brenda was feeling well enough, she told me that she had experienced the afterlife; the spiritual realm. Everyone around her was dressed in white, flowing garb, and apparently, I was there. She told me that my face bore none of the wrinkles with which she had become so familiar, and that she couldn't stop staring at me, thinking I looked like I was only twenty-six years old. Perhaps, this was a projection of the age of my soul, or a reflection of my energetic age, as our bodies may age but our spirits live on without the trappings of time. Brenda was given the choice, while in that white-light realm, to either stay on earth, or move onwards to the afterlife. She told me that I stopped her before she could answer, saying,

No. You come back. I will do it. ***I'll do it.*** *I will get us through. I promised you a Temple marriage, and you're gonna get it. And I'll keep this family together.*

She told me the spirits made sure she knew how hard her recovery was going to be; how hard it was *all* going to be. The poor thing, she really has been through it all. And even this long road of recovery wasn't the end of her struggles - not nearly. But she is still here, and she fights hard. It took about a year for the swelling in Brenda's abdomen to go down enough for her to have reconstructive surgery. Thankfully, that surgery went well, and was very successful all around.

My insurance company called me one day, wanting to know if there was any chance of malpractice. I began getting letters, around that same time, prompting me to get legal help if there was any chance of a malpractice suit. My insurance company, which was through work, had paid out over a million dollars in insurance premiums over that year and a half after the first surgery. And of *course* it was malpractice - it was gross malpractice.

I decided to go for it, and boy, did I have some great attorneys. I had only one referral, to a law practice out of Little Rock, Arkansas, and I signed with them immediately.

Once Brenda was well enough, we went to federal court in Memphis. And I may say "well", but she really has never been the same since. She still has problems, to this day, because of that surgery… but at least she's put back together, now.

Well, we fought and won the malpractice suit, and I could finally exhale just a little bit, since I had a cushion of money to work with, to help support the family and use to pay off bills.

It was exciting, learning about the whole legal process and all, but I never would have wished those experiences on myself. Crazy enough, though, the foreman of the jury in our courtroom was a Mormon. If you can believe it! What are the chances? There are very few Mormons down south. It was a big help to us, in any case, as the jury foreman was able to inform the jury about the Mormon support system, the Mormon relief society, what a ward is, as well as how people band together to help one another out whenever something drastic occurs, and all of that.

Things can happen for the best, in the craziest of ways.

CHAPTER NINE

The Trial in the Court of Public Opinion: 2015 – 2016

One Saturday afternoon, a few months after Brenda had come home from the hospital, I was in the kitchen with a Bluetooth in my ear. I had the baby, Ilana, in my left arm, and was on my knees putting pots and pans up under the dish counter with my right, when my phone rang. It was a seventeen-year-old member of the community named Michael. He called me and said,

Keith, I'm gay… and I want to know if you will be with me, so I can see if I like it.

I couldn't believe it! I immediately froze, stopped where I was: crouched, with one arm bent under the sink, the other trying to support Ilana. Brenda and I had been married for over eleven years by this point, and from the moment we'd said *I do*, I hadn't looked back. Not to that stage of my life, and definitely not to that part of myself.

I absolutely love my current life. I love being active in church, and having a family, and the babies… which is exactly why it was so easy for me to deal with whatever I needed to when it came to Brenda's illness. Because, I *love* my life. I love it that much. Love it now like I loved it then. And I didn't want to have come so far, only to go backwards. I didn't want to have to deal with [or even think about] these things I'd already dealt with; already worked through. Especially because, in so doing, I would break the covenant that Brenda and I had made in the Temple when we first got married.

I went into the other room and shout-whispered into the phone:

Michael, listen to me. You're not gay. You don't even know anything about that… and, besides, who told you about all this? …referring to his knowledge of my past sexuality.

The older members of my family would know about my past, you know, of course. But it'd been so long... so many years since all that. Now I was a daddy, and a husband, and loyally so. Michael replied, saying,

My dad. That's why he doesn't like you.

I said back into the phone, *Well, forget about your dad. No, I will not be with you. Are you insane? I'm not going to Parchman (Mississippi State Penitentiary) for you, or for anyone, only to have some other guy end up raising my kids. Do **not** call back here again with that garbage!*

And then he persisted again, saying, **Please?**

I said, **WHAT? No. Don't** *call back over here with that mess.*

And then we hung up.

After that, I was really angry with him. Even still, I didn't go tattling on him.

My mind went directly back to when I was his age. I knew it would cause needless drama, so I never thought to call his mother, Tiffany. Plus, that part of my life was so far behind me, I didn't really want to dredge it all back up!

I remembered what it was like to be his age; hormones boiling over and all. You go crazy, and don't know who you are or how to act. *Heck*, I'd been messing around with it even at fourteen, and here he was seventeen; nearly an adult.

Later on, I would come to find out that he actually had been experimenting and messing around since the same age as I had: fourteen; around puberty. Regardless, I just couldn't believe that he was really gay. I never would've guessed.

I didn't hear another peep out of him about it after that. He would come around whenever the family was over [since they were basically counted as family], and sometimes - if he was drinking or something - I would notice him giving me the eye, but he really did leave me alone and didn't try anything stupid. Plus, I figured that if he really was gay, it was probably just some sort of youthful fantasy, to be with an older guy like that. Basically, I knew where he was coming from, but I still couldn't really talk to him, or even look at him during that time, for fear of encouraging unwanted attention.

When he was nearly nineteen, he started calling me again. I was adamant, saying, *no, no, no*... like a scratched CD, but he persisted ruthlessly. He would say,

I'm legal now, and I know you used to do that, so will you be with me?

The first time he called, I didn't have any money, so I knew he wasn't after money. He's just gay, and that's really it.

Well, remember that I was still taking care of Brenda all this time, and was exhausted from the nearly two years of constant run around. All my brain could think about every day was the continuous cycle of laundry, nursing, Brenda, the kids, school, cooking, cleaning, yard work, and so on… I was frankly too exhausted to give a darn about this young boy's propositions. I really just wanted him to leave me alone, so I could focus on all that I already had going on.

I mean, I had *enough* going on at the time already, obviously. I did not ask for this, and I sure didn't want it. In looking back, I should have considered moving away right then, but that thought never crossed my mind. I loved my family and community unconditionally, and it never even entered my mind to move away from them.

So for about six months, he would just call and call and call, always a new script with the same material. *Please. Please, nobody will ever find out.* Well, if that wasn't the Devil himself, trying to tempt me with the same trials of old. I just kept on the same track, saying, *no, no, no…* and hoping he would give up. But he wouldn't; he didn't.

Then, after months and months of calling, I suddenly found myself back in my old life. I was having a particularly difficult week with the balancing act that was my life, and it all just got to me. I crumbled under the weight of temptation. I gave in.

During the time, I had begun to drink a little bit, to cope with it all. I mean, I didn't have anyone, really, to speak to or share my struggles with. I felt such a distance between Brenda and I, both because of her illness and my responsibilities. As a result of all this, my defenses were lowered.

After I crossed the line, I *completely* flipped out, because I knew that I had broken my Temple covenants to Brenda. I became super depressed. Especially knowing that someday I would have to come clean to her, in order to maintain the Temple Marriage we'd worked so hard to build up over the years. On top of this, I didn't really have a vocal relationship with Brenda at the time, so the thought of burdening her already overburdened spirit with this information just destroyed me.

I knew that, someday, I was gonna have to break Brenda's heart, and with that, go through the repentance process, and the church's system, to even deserve her again. You cannot be married in the Temple after being unfaithful, without repentance. And the Temple was what I wanted, so I knew I was gonna do whatever it took.

Never, at any time, did I want to ditch my family, or go back to the gay life, or anything even remotely of the sort.

I was scared to death; shaking in my boots at the thought of losing all that I had worked so hard to build [and then rebuild!]. But I guess that's the thing with any Temple. When it needs maintenance, you work on it. When it crumbles, you rebuild it; only, stronger than before.

After I crossed the line that first time, it was too late. What had been done could not be undone. I knew that telling Brenda, no matter how, when or where, would be a big mess. I mean, we had children now… we had been through so much together… and she was *just* beginning to feel like herself again. I felt just awful about it all.

So, I thought, *well, someday… but… not* **today**.

Of course, Michael kept calling, wanting to get together. And as I'd already crossed the line, and wasn't ready to be honest with Brenda, I was able to put it out of my mind, hoping it would just go away until the day when I could once again handle my own dirty laundry.

I'm not saying that this was right. It's just how I felt, and what I decided at the time. And it wasn't like I ever went looking for anything with him; not ever.

I was so overwhelmed with what life had been throwing my way that I allowed it to occur one or two more times before, really, I became his confidant, and nothing more. I listened to his escapades, helped him out when he had a small fender bender, and did what I could to support him. In a way, he was like my mid-life crisis after all I'd been through.

As I've said, I consider same-sex attraction to be a trial you must overcome, rather than a defining characteristic, and this guy turned out to be quite the trial for me, when I was already so downtrodden from life.

I want to emphasize: only because my SSA was such a large part of my past, was it so easy for me to fall back into the lifestyle. Though I've changed and grown so much since then, old habits can die hard. I was able to block out how wrong it was temporarily, because as I said early on, I have always been comfortable in my own skin no matter what was going on in my life, able to shut it all out to deal with later.

After the intimate interaction ended, I was exhausted, really. I didn't know what to do; I felt like I couldn't handle taking even one more step. I still had all my responsibilities with the kids and taking care of Brenda. My priority was in protecting her physical and mental health.

I figured my shenanigans would have absolutely crushed her, potentially having a negative effect on her physical health. However, she always surprises me; she's always so much stronger than I give her credit for. Further confirmation, I know, that she is meant to be my eternal companion. Looking back, she may have been able to handle it, but my gut told me it wasn't yet the time.

And meanwhile, The Adversary was tempting me even further. There were guys all over me, everywhere I went, from the moment I had broken my covenant. The devil was on my back, trying to pull me away from my true north. Wherever I went, some guy was giving me the eye... I went to the gym one day, and some dude crawled *in the shower* with me! Completely unsolicited!

I thought, *What in the **hell** is going on around here!?*

Well, I did know what was going on, and it was *hell*, indeed: Satan trying to tempt me at every turn.

I figured that once Michael went off to college or something, he would move on with his life in some way or another, and the whole thing would be behind me for good. I knew that, when that time came, I would be able to tell Brenda about it, and deal with the consequences of my actions without distractions.

Sure enough, the whole relationship played itself out quickly, and I tried my best to just look after him while it was going on. We talked a lot, and we were able to communicate well, since I understood where he was coming from. I became his confidant, and often told him that if he could choose at all, being married with a family was the way to the most happiness.

I felt bad for him: I knew he was going to have a hard time figuring himself out, and especially so with that family of his. They weren't very religious, and they were very dramatic. He said over and over,

They won't love me if they find out.

I tried to convince him otherwise, since I had never felt any animosity from them myself, growing up.

[But this was before I knew they were all a little crazy.]

Michael was quite the temptation for me. I'm not really going to go into it, but let me just say, it was quite adventuresome, and quite different from what I'd experienced in the eighties. At least, to me it was all new! Which made it easier to do, in some ways, but also easier to push away, after the initial shock and excitement wore off.

The thing most people don't understand is just how free the gay lifestyle is. Promiscuity is a part of the culture: non-committal and often without heavy emotional connection. Like my mother, who never left behind the mindset cage she'd inherited from her upbringing in Sledge, MS, so many people judge the world based only in what they've been exposed to or experienced firsthand. So I don't blame those who can't wrap their minds around the lifestyle. How can you ever really know what you've not experienced?

The cousins and kids who were Michael's age would come over to my house, and sometimes I would catch them smoking in the backyard, or whatever of the sort. They felt comfortable around me, because I didn't tattle on them, and I didn't give them any sort of a hard time about who they were or what they were up to. Plus, I figured they were going to smoke anyway, no matter what I said, and at least this way they were safe and around an adult they could trust.

I always felt that, if these kids ever got into real trouble, they would need somewhere else to go, other than to their parents'. I got many of those kids out of trouble without their parents even knowing it. Nothing major that violates the parent-child bond, just some minor stumbles like what most kids experience. When I was that age, I had an aunt I could turn to when I was worried my own parents couldn't understand, and I have always looked back, grateful for it.

My Aunt Peggy would always loan me some money if I was ever short, and she even cosigned a loan when I needed a new car; but what meant the most was how she was always so accepting and supportive of whatever I felt, rather than condemning what she didn't approve of or understand. She just wanted to make sure that I was safe, and didn't much bother with all the rest. I felt like maybe these kids needed the same: somebody neutral and supportive to go to in times of need.

Now, maybe I didn't get into the same kind of "trouble", per se, as some of these kids, but all youth is trouble, really. All youth is pushing boundaries, and making claim to the extremes of a personality; stretching into the unexplored places to find self-understanding and acceptance.

Hanging around these kids brought my guard down even moreso, I guess. It was hard to push back with Michael, especially while this was all going on. I almost wonder whether the relationship would've dissipated even more quickly if the kids weren't over so often, but what's passed is past.

I feel guilt for breaking my covenants. I feel guilt for putting Brenda in the position to feel more pain, especially when I promised her that I wouldn't. However, I choose not to let this guilt fill me up. I look to this experience as another lesson learned while here on Earth. I will use this lesson, and not make the same mistake twice.

Sin is sin, and can take many forms, but I will not roll on the floor crying, feeling sorry for myself and what I've done. I know who I am, and I *know* how the adversary likes to interject in our vulnerabilities at the precise moment when our defenses are down.

I'm still here. Brenda is still here. We have children to raise, and there is always room for growth. I just hope that my experiences can help others see how their journey is just that: a journey. Perfection is scarce in this life, and as humans *we make mistakes*. We just do. We can try our hardest to attain perfection, and we can beat ourselves up for making the wrong decisions, but we are sure to stumble in our attempts. It is up to each of us how we handle our stumbles.

This is the advice I gave the youth hanging around our house. I hoped to help these kids avoid some of the pain of their own discovery phases, so they could find their way faster and without such sorrows.

I also told them, as I would tell anyone, to establish some absolutes in your life, other than yourself. Then, to relax about it, hold firm to those absolutes, and do whatever you can to bring yourself closer to the Heavenly Father. When the hard times come, then you can hold on to what you know; what you've established, and you'll have the eternal support of the Father.

Balance, and find one or two friends who are going to lead you the right way. Then you can be yourself, but also work on yourself while feeling supported. Learn what you can along the way, and ask for help when you need it! If you do, you are sure to attract the right people to help you along your way.

Alma 32:27 says,

If ye will awake and arouse your faculties, even to experiment upon my words, and exercise a particle of faith, yea, even if ye can no more than desire to believe, let this desire work in you, even until ye believe in a manner that ye can give place for a portion of my words.

To me, this says that if one wants to believe, that is enough. The mere desire to believe will grow inside of you, so long as you remain humble to it. Anything you want can be brought into this life, so long as you make it an absolute in your journey, and nurture it until it comes to life.

CHAPTER TEN
Family Affairs: 2015 – 2016

Michael's mother, Tiffany, you may remember from earlier on in the story. If you can recall when I called home to Mississippi, just after Ethan was born, to tell my family all about his arrival, the girl who first answered the phone was Tiffany.

Well, this is her. And Michael is her second child.

She's always been a controlling mother. And not just your regular, run-of-the-mill helicopter parent. No. Tiffany has four children, and there were always issues between she and her kids.

Tiffany thought Michael was doing something behind her back regarding his sexuality. She later said that she "knew he was", so she hired a private detective to follow him.

Over the course of one year, she paid out over *fifty thousand dollars* to this private investigator - and she is no rich woman. She was working extra shifts, and paid the man out of her own pocket just to see what her son was up to.

She, apparently, wanted to confirm whether or not he was gay, and she wanted to find out what on earth he was doing hanging around me so much. So she had us followed.

I'm sorry, but that's two illegal actions in one fail swoop. It is against the law to have somebody followed, and it is against the law to read private messages. Gross invasion of privacy is a civil tort. A large chunk of the money she paid to those private detectives was spent on acquiring Michael's text messages *without* a court order, which included the stream of messages between Michael and I.

What she did was not only illegal, but a *total* invasion of privacy.

She claims that she didn't know he was gay, but I know that's a lie, because he never had any girlfriends, and had kept evidence of his interests in the house where Tiffany lived with him. I know that there's *no way* she was so in the dark. Plus, if she didn't know he was gay, why was she so worried about his hanging out with me?

All of this makes me wonder…. There's gotta be something more to the story, that she is either guilty of, or hiding from. There must be some reason why she would want to go to those lengths to have him followed. Reasons more than that she was mortified he might be gay.

All in all, she didn't even find out much of anything; especially as the relationship had dissipated somewhat quickly, and Michael and I were both on our own paths by the time she even had any information about it at all. Mostly, Michael just came around to hang out and have someone he could relate to. I sometimes wonder whether that's why he tracked me down and trolled me: an immature attempt at finding someone he could relate to. As I said, he could confide in me and we did a lot of talking about his future.

Now, I grew up with Tiffany. She was basically a part of the family, and I always loved her, without reservation. I trusted her, without fail. She was one of the people who had rallied around me when Brenda was so ill. Her entire family had encouraged and loved me every minute of my youth, never turning away from my sexuality, nor condemning or judging me without explanation.

I *loved* these people. There's nothing they could've done, that I wouldn't have stood up for them for. We were not only good friends, but neighbors, as well.

I was so blinded by my love for them, and was always happy to be around them all. Previous to this, I had never felt estranged from them for my sexuality, struggles, or any of it. And when I decided to move my family back to Mississippi after Ethan was born to be closer to them all, they were there for me, and helped me. I loved them, and all I wanted was to be nearer to them.

They loved me back, but now, I see that was only on a superficial level, and only until something occurred that was beyond their control.

Just before this all went down, we had even invested in land with them. My aunt, uncle, myself, and a few family friends [including Tiffany] had all split the bill to buy up this forty-acre plot of land, upon which we were all going to build ourselves new houses, so that we could live even closer to one another.

How lucky we were to get out of that at the last minute!

I have to say, I was warned by people in the neighborhood, and the community, that they were a little crazy. And I had been away for years, so perhaps I should've listened a bit to those forewarnings. Plus, now that I've removed the rose-colored glasses from my eyes, and am recalling the events of the past, I've come to find several instances of their instability. I've come to realize that there were some definite cracks in the pavement, that were never there before I'd moved back to live close to them again. Even my cousin Robyn regularly talked about these people like dogs, and she was so close with them all. No honor among thieves, so to speak.

So, anyways. On June 10th of 2016, they received the official transcript of text messages, and she and her husband *absolutely flipped out*. The text messages confirmed that her son was, indeed, gay; that he had had interactions with me; and just as well with others; and they also found out about all of his paraphernalia and fetishes: everything. Imagine, just *imagine* having your parents pay $50,000 to find out your every dirty little secret!

Tiffany's younger brother, Adam, called me and wanted to know what was going on. I told him the flat-out truth, and he said, *Well, they're coming to your house, so you'd better leave.*

I instantly knew: we had to go. We had to get out.

I had to - within fifteen minutes - tell Brenda what had been going on, get the kids together, get the dogs, and get going. I knew there was gonna be a scene, and all I could focus on was Getting My Family Out, and getting to safety. I didn't want my kids to see that mess; especially my ten-year-old. Even to this day, they don't really know what happened. I've always tried to protect them from that kind of drama.

My neighbors called about an hour after we'd left the house and told me what was going on after we left: they said,

There was a scene like you have never seen before; not even like what you would see on the Jerry Springer show.

Michael's dad came up on my yard with an axe, and immediately started chopping up one of my cars. Tiffany was screaming and crying and falling all over the yard, collapsing and clawing herself.

I knew that it was over, that we wouldn't be able to come back, and that my kids wouldn't be able to play with their cousins everyday anymore. It was obvious that Tiffany and her husband wanted to completely push us out of our family, and that Tiffany felt she had the right.

Tiffany and her husband were [according to our family and friends] worried it was all gonna blow over, and that we'd try to retie our family bonds and push *them* out, which was apparently why they overreacted in my front yard. But, no doubt, I knew it was over. I knew it wouldn't ever blow over.

They didn't wait for any explanation, no. They automatically became aggressive when the relationship came to light, without any sense of patience or understanding. They used deceit to attack. Were my son involved in such a situation, I know it would hurt, and it would hurt bad. But, I would wait with patience in my heart, until I knew and understood what had really happened. Of course, Ethan is a little ladies man already, brushing his teeth each morning "for the girls..." but, regardless.

The thing is, I didn't go after Michael; he came after me. I never would have actively pursued such a thing. Never in a million years did I consider trolling some young adult. It was never on my mind, and I had absolutely no agenda. It happened, as life does. I messed up in how I handled it, as humans do. And yet, they choose to blame me completely, and force me out of my own home.

I wanted to handle my own dirty laundry on my own terms, anyway. I was not about to let that family decide where I was gonna live.

Sadly, I'm told Tiffany tried causing herself harm over this. She tried to jump out of a moving car, and was then hospitalized and sedated. A whole hell of a lot to put yourself through, all because your son is gay and acted on it, if you ask me. Perhaps they just didn't want him to be gay, or wanted someone to blame for his actions… or perhaps they really enjoy drama. Who's to know?

I just know there has got to be more to the story. I mean, Michael may very well be just like me: a little confused, navigating his own journey, and all he really needs is space. And when I was going through the very same when I was younger, Tiffany was never judgmental, nor unsupportive.

It just doesn't make sense.

She just had to have put herself through such pain for a lot more personal of reasons than his sexuality, or the relationship; ones that I'll probably never know or understand. Frankly, I don't need to. But I will pray that her son makes it out alright.

They would love to believe that I turned Michael gay. Please. Give me a break. I don't even *have* that kind of firepower. And as laid back as I'm so known to be, why would I even bother? I've got everything I ever wanted. All I want now is to move forward, past the mistake I made, and get right with my covenant once more.

After we left the house, with as much packed into the car as we could fit, we decided to go to Waco, TX. We stayed at a Hilton while discussing where we could go from there. I knew we'd have to move, but I also knew I didn't want to be with those people anymore, so I didn't mind so much.

They wouldn't let up. Even when we came back about a month later to load up all of our stuff, we had to block the windows and make it look all dark, because Tiffany's husband was still stalking us. We had to go under the cover of night to get all of our stuff! But I couldn't let anything happen in front of my kids; I had to be cool with that, and keep it together as best as I could.

Michael's parents, in the meantime, had told everybody down there - *all our family and friends* - that we agreed to leave so they would not prosecute us; which is a total delusion on their part. Believe me, if there was any way they could blame me and have me in jail, they would - I'd already be there now. And if I had done something illegal, they would've already seen to it that I be held responsible to the max.

Michael has taken absolutely no responsibility. It's immature, but I understand his plight completely. Even though they're a bit much, they're all the family he has, and he had to deny what went down to survive. [Even though they have his text messages, showing everything in black and white, they still choose to believe that it was all my fault; that I did it all.] Not that I blame him, nor anybody else, for my part. I take full ownership for my mistakes, and am ready to be responsible for them, making amends wherever possible.

I have spoken with Michael once since all the drama ensued. I begged him to go to into the service or something to get away from his family - because, likely, they will never come to understand him - but he chose not to. I only hope that he is doing well, and making the best of his situation.

By invading his privacy, Michael's parents absolutely shredded his relationship with not only them, but his entire extended family, our family, and the community. And now, his words keep coming back to me... *They won't love me if they find out.* Well, it's obviously all out now, and I just hope he navigates it alright.

And Tiffany must have been pretty confident that I wouldn't come and kick *her* door in or take a hatchet to *her* car, when she set those private investigators after me and illegally read my private messages. I guess that's what being so laid back gets you; anyone who knows me knows I don't care to make drama out of a mess.

On the road to Waco, Brenda was clawing at herself in frustration and upset.

She said, *You promised.*

I didn't know what to say. All I could say was,

*I'm sorry. I never meant to get back into that lifestyle. I don't want it. I've come too far, and I love my kids, and I don't want to go and have any boyfriends. I want **you**. I just gave in that one time, and then it got out of hand and I didn't know how to get out of it or tell you. I panicked.*

It was several weeks before I could really get her to calm down after that. I wanted to keep her out of the hospital above all else. I knew we would get down to the bottom of everything with time, but I wanted to ensure that my actions didn't affect her health.

We have seen counselors since then, and everything is great between the two of us; we're doing fine. It took a few months, but we were able to communicate, and refocus on our kids and marriage despite the mistakes. And now, everything is out in the open. I mean, Brenda and I had never even discussed SSA in depth until now. And as we've delved into such details, we have only become closer.

I know she felt betrayed by me, and I know she felt blindsided by my actions. I never wanted that for her. I had wanted to tell her on our own time, and when she was well enough to take it. I wanted to break it to her gently, when I knew she could absorb the shock of it all. But, I wasn't given that time, no.

I will never get that close to it again, because like I said I've gone too far, and I've come too far. I've come *far* too far to be fooling around with these queens, and I'm just upset that I got sucked into it at all; that I *let* myself sink back in to those old habits. And that's where Brenda and I are aligned in understanding: we've both come too far, together, and we are each other's eternal partner. We have struggled too much and worked too hard together in determination to be with our Heavenly Father, to give up now. No matter what it takes, we will keep fighting.

This just goes to show about temptation though, and how The Adversary will catch you at your lowest point.

I mean, I was so beat down after two years of worrying and caring for my family like a madman, that I was weakened, and my defenses were all down. Being mentally separated from Brenda during her illness weakened my defenses and made me feel so lonely. I know that's a part of it. And I know we each struggle with our own form of temptation. Some of us are quick to anger, aggression or violence, much like Tiffany and her husband. Others of us are tempted by desires we don't really want to pursue. We each must persevere through these challenges; these trials that we face. But we absolutely must fight for what we most want, because the road to evil is paved with good intentions, and The Adversary is quite true to his name.

I gained the confidence to face one trial after another through the work I had done when I was young. Studying the scriptures taught me *how* to persevere, which prepared me for the experiences I faced later on in life, such as the surgery and relationship. I knew how to take care of my family and put my own needs aside, because I knew God's love would do the same for me. And even when I broke my covenant, he still didn't allow me to forget what I most desired, and helped me piece back together the life that *I* wanted; the life I feel the Lord truly intended for me to lead. And now, it's stronger than ever.

I knew that the gospel was true, and so I held on tight to that truth through it all.

I always knew who I was and what my priorities were, but only through deciding *not* to rebel against the religious aspect of my life did I find the divine help I needed to persevere the trials I faced.

Had I not persevered, I never would've found everything I've always wanted, and without the strength the Lord gave me, I would never have known how to fight for it all.

In the LDS church, when you have a transgression like mine, such as breaking your Temple covenants, you attend what I call the *Court of Love*. And it really is; I felt only loving support from their guidance. They decided that I should be disfellowshipped from the church and have my Temple blessings suspended for one year, while I repented and slowly regained my deservance.

This year was sort of like a reset button, for which I am grateful. Those poor guys though. As I told my story, I'm sure they were hearing a mess the likes of which they had never heard before!

Initially, in telling my Bishop what was up, he questioned my sincerity in repentance. He asked me whether I was there because I had gotten caught, or because I was truly repentant.

My sin was in direct conflict with the covenants I made with my family. The relationship sure threw a wrench in my plans, as my SSA has seemed to do with my entire life journey, but I know it was for a reason. I'm not proud of my mistakes, but I know, that when I work to rebuild what I have broken, the potential exists to make things better and stronger than ever before.

Having a full understanding of the Gospel, and the necessary steps involved in ridding one's self of transgression in order to re-enter the Temple, I never felt the need to [as I had described to the Bishop] "roll on the floor crying" to convince him of my regret. Again, no one understands the *Atonement of Christ* as I have learned through the Prophet Joseph Smith. I understood from the beginning what I needed to do, and I was happy to do the work, and get the process behind me, so I could enter the Temple again.

I know Brenda was saved for me. Without her, I wouldn't have any of this. I wouldn't have an eternal family to rebuild, for which I am grateful. I am grateful that my mishaps have brought us closer together than ever before. I am grateful she knows and accepts more about me now than ever, and I am grateful that I know what I know to be true, in my heart, well enough to know the right steps to take, to get back on track with what I most desire in my heart.

This past year has opened up Brenda's and my perception of how best to raise our kids, as well. We have forged a better understanding of how to prepare our kids for the roads that lay ahead of them, and the bumps they are sure to experience along the way. We have focused on our family prayers, and as always, instill the light of God's love in their hearts, every chance we get.

Throughout this time of disfellowshipment, I've stuck closely to the passage from John 6:67, where Jesus says to the disciples,

Will ye go away also?

I will not go away. I will never leave the Temple of the Lord.

I have to just move on and not get upset about the process of getting back to the Temple... If Joseph Smith saw what he said he saw, where else shall we go but to the Temple? And what else shall we do but traverse every trial that falls before us on our way there?

As penance, I was also unable to partake of the Lord's supper until Thanksgiving of 2017, about when this book will be released. But I am back on track, have remained devout to my repentance, and this Thanksgiving will be able to go back to the Temple and walk humbly once more in the light of the Lord's grace.

You know, I've always tried to protect Brenda from all this garbage. I never told her the gory details of my youth, and never really dug into all these details at all, because I was still so immature during those times, and Brenda was the real deal, and I knew that.

She's far better than me in nearly every way, and I had enough sense to know to marry up and work my butt off to be better; to be worthy of the Temple.

I never wanted Brenda to have to go through any more pain, and I always wished to be able to protect her from any garbage related to my own personal trials. Those whole eleven years, through the surgery and the relationship, I always tried to protect her from outside influences about any shenanigans.

When you're married in the Temple, it's for eternity.

Brenda understands the covenants, and I'm grateful for that. Our kids need both of us in the home, and she is a strong enough woman to get past a transgression, work through it with her partner, and know that her testimony is strong enough to get her through anything. She is the woman I always wanted; always dreamt of. She wasn't going to let the adversary, nor her husband's demons, break up her eternal family.

She is stronger than I expect, at every turn.

When she struggled with the aftermath of her surgery, I was her strength. I was even, apparently, up there in the clouds with her, telling her to come on back and persevere with me. When I stumbled, fell, and broke my covenants with her, she didn't shut the door in my face. Unlike the rest of my extended family and friends in Mississippi, she stood by me and had the patience and faith to pull me back in, and rebuild the Temple Marriage with me from the ground up. She understands me, and accepts me for who I am, which is further proof that she was saved for me.

And as I said before, now we're stronger than ever. Funny, how things work that way.

CHAPTER ELEVEN

Utah: 2016 – Present

So, we ended up in Salt Lake City, Utah: my wife's homeland.

Initially, we stayed with a friend while deciding where to live. Brenda and I continued to see a counselor to work on our marriage, and all the while I've been embracing the stages of repentance. As well, I immediately fell straight back into my old habit of studying the scriptures and doctrinal books intensely. I'd done it all my life, whenever I found myself needing help or seeking comfort.

We were able to get the kids set up with a school easily enough, since it was still the end of summer when we got to Utah, and I got a job almost instantly. You see, doing what I do, I'm quite easily able to get a job almost anywhere. [Part of the appeal for me…]

Though it was quite a shift for our children, they've adjusted really well. The culture we're in now is completely and totally different from where they grew up in Mississippi. They have far more opportunities here than they did before. And though they aren't able to play with so many cousins as they used to, we now live in the same city as Ethan's parents and siblings, as well a large chunk of mine and Brenda's extended family.

My life is so wonderful. As you may recall, I always loved keeping a clean room as a kid, but when I see my kids' messy bedrooms, or find a wet towel on the bathroom floor, all I can do is smile. I am *their* father. The miracles that got me here are so much more important than any of this… than absolutely anything else. I am so grateful every day for it.

Ethan is in the All Stars baseball league, and he takes piano lessons. He is very athletic, and he *is* gonna play football for BYU if it's the last thing I do! I took him to Trump's Inauguration, and it was the coolest thing! To be there, with my boy… I am blessed! Ilana is starting to grow up as well, and is all set up to take dance lessons soon, which we're really excited about.

Plus, we're just that much closer to Hawaii now, so hey!

We started attending church again after the move, and have been in two wards since. They've both been so great, and such good communities to be immersed in.

When we drove up with the moving van, the Elders Quorum descended upon us uninvited, and helped us unload. Our Ward consists of about eight city blocks, now.

Just after we made the move, I began filing a suit against Michael's parents [since everything they did was illegal], but I dropped the case once life threw us yet another curveball.

The attorney I met with briefly, while opening a case against them, confirmed that my actions were all within the law, while also bringing up a perspective that made me think a bit further into my family's motivations. He said,

There just has to be more reason behind her actions. There has to be more to it than that she wanted to know whether her son was gay. Was there some abuse? Was she guilty about something? People don't pay $50,000, and break all these laws, just to see if their son is gay.

That family only cares about how they appear to others. They don't *really* care about Michael, or else they wouldn't have gone about things the way they did; they *certainly* don't care about me, and aren't worried about my filing suit against their irreprehensible actions; and they sure don't give any cares that my kids had to be uprooted and moved to a new school over this. They only care about themselves. Tiffany would pay $50,000 to expose a secret, but wouldn't ever pay a cent for damages. So much drama and deterioration.

I wish to have *my* day in court with my family, as it were. Or, at least, I used to wish it. Now I don't really want anything to do with those blood relatives who turned away from me when the relationship came to light. To be honest, I can no longer grant them the term of family, as it is one of endearment; and one that I think has to be earned. I am happy to be out of the asylum; free of the judgments and disdain, and wish for others to be cautious if they come into contact with these people.

So often in life, we cannot have our way, no matter how we try, and must navigate regardless. So often, we have to move on without closure, and without any sensible resolution. Since arriving in Utah, I've come to realize that if something terrible were to happen to me, my children would never really know who I was. They need to hear it from me personally. Additionally, my ten-year-old, Ethan is so inquisitive about my childhood years, and I wouldn't want to deprive him of that insight.

I am happy to be out of the asylum, but Michael is still there, surrounded by individuals that will never understand him. I hope he never becomes depressed, nor has any untoward effects because of his screeching lunatic of a mother, who threw down the curtain on his life - unlawfully - and has actually shredded his relationship with his entire extended family. Yet another reason the event absolutely had to be documented. Michael does not deserve all this backlash. For this reason and others, I will always be his advocate.

Tiffany is the head of the asylum, and as of yet, no one has been willing or able to wrest control of the family, including her younger brother: a situation that I am plenty happy to be free from. Again, until this event, I would have never even dreamt of leaving. I just couldn't see their true selves before.

Everyone is entitled to their privacy and the ability to handle their own lives. Even people with SSA.

Now, back to that curve ball I mentioned earlier; the reason I decided to drop my lawsuit against those people:

This past October (2016), Brenda needed another surgery.

Poor girl still had fibroids growing all the way to her back, causing her a lot of lower back pains. The doctors were never able to fix the original issue, and so she's struggled with her endometriosis ever since, while also trying to heal.

So, we went back to the hospital in Memphis for another surgery, to better close the muscles in her stomach, to take a piece of mesh out that was still in there, and to perform a complete hysterectomy [as a means of finally nipping her endometriosis in the bud].

The kids were in school, and some friends watched them otherwise, while we were away. We went to Memphis, once again thinking that this would be a short two weeks away [two weeks because it was still quite a major surgery].

Well, she ended up on the ventilator once again, clinging to her life. This time for about a week. I stayed until it looked like she was okay, but then the minute I would leave, she would seemingly tank. She was in respiratory distress, and also had contracted an acute form of MS called ADEM, where the myelin sheath of some of the nerves in your brain lose their covering. Well, her sheath is gone.

When I walked in, expecting her to be better, there she was, babbling away, saying *ba ba ba…*

I thought, *What in the heck is this now? Not again.*

After having septic shock that first time for almost a year, her immune system was still so trashed that it couldn't handle everything having the operation did to her body.

There I was, though, in that hospital, all alone, all those weekends, thinking, *There we go. I'm gonna lose her, again. I'm right back here…*

Things always tend to go through your mind at those moments; things you would never think about otherwise. The cynic inside me rose up at that moment, thinking, *Heavenly Father let us keep her a few more years, so that she could raise the baby girl she'd always wanted, and now he's gonna try to take her away again.*

I was just a wreck; a *wreck.*

So I stayed until she was well enough, and then traveled back to Utah to see the kids. But then, when I got back to Utah, I received word that she had crashed again. I ended up going back and forth between Memphis and Salt Lake City like this seven weekends in a row. And each time that I'd get back to Utah, expecting her health to keep getting better and better, I would again receive word that her system had crashed. So, off I would go, back to Memphis.

Finally, she started getting better, and spent some time in rehab before coming home. I was able to bring her back home by Christmas last year, thankfully.

A friend of mine came out here to Utah, to help me with the kids. I needed someone that I could trust, since I had all these different people picking up and dropping off my kids, and I needed just one person I trusted. So that was a great help!

Brenda had to be on oxygen for about six weeks after she got home, due to respiratory distress. Then, one day around Christmas after she'd come home from the hospital, at around four pm in the afternoon, she said to me,

I think I may have a UTI.

By ten pm that night, she was flat on her back in the ICU, with a Levophed drip to keep her alive. She had gone septic *again*, making this the third time she'd had septic shock. She was fighting for her life, *again*.

She's doing well now, thankfully.

Well, now here again, with Brenda fighting for her life, I had so much going on that I decided to drop the lawsuit against Tiffany and her family. Plus, I didn't really want to have to go back and engage with those people, even if it was in a courtroom. To be honest, I didn't even really trust them to behave with a judge present!

However, we are well within the statute of limitations regarding *witnessed* destruction and theft of private property, invasion of privacy, obtaining text messages without a court order, and prosecution under federal hate crime legislation. Just saying…

But, I decided a book would be better. I wanted my kids to understand the troubles that I went through for them. I didn't want to leave room for any miscommunication about my life, should anything happen to me. And I didn't want, someday, for that part of the family to start telling my kids about their perspective of me, and skew me in their eyes. No. I couldn't trust in that.

We, of course, have not had any contact with those folks back in Mississippi, and probably never will again. My relatives have bought up all Tiffany's lies, and sold them all around again. They have continued to smear my name and spread their own brand of lies to make themselves out to be the victims, ever since we left. But having a gay son does not make them victims, and I did not prey on their son.

All they needed to do was call me… and perhaps we could've worked it all out. After all, I did not commit murder. I did nothing illegal. I know that what I did was wrong in some ways, but that is between me and my family, and me and Michael. No one else should've ever gotten involved.

Things do work out for the best, though. Back then, nothing would've ripped me away from that part of the family. Now that I can see the truth, though, I'm so thankful we didn't get too far in the preparations to build that new house. I would have lost a lot of money, as well as the family and friends who are now estranged from my life.

We were able to sell our part of the land quite quickly, actually. And then, just about a month after we moved, we left our friend's place and began renting an apartment. In August of last year (2016), we started renting, and then, this summer, we were able to finally buy a house of our own!

We're all so happy now; it's so great out here in Utah. Sometimes, it's nice to weed your garden of the things that are no good for you.

Sidney Sperry was a scholar at BYU back in the 50's. His writings about the restored gospel are riveting. And that's why I'm here, and I know it, and I don't care who else does know it.

I'm not trying to tell anybody how to live or what to believe. If you wanna be gay, go do it, whatever… But as for me, in my life, every time I've chosen to humble myself, or have made myself available to the Holy Spirit [no matter what lifestyle I was living], there was always help there for me.

The message is: no matter what religion, race, or lifestyle, rejoice because you are known, personally, by our Heavenly Father. *Personally.*

CONCLUSION

Moving Forward, to a Bright Future

Had I continued with my old life, I wouldn't have my wife or

kids. It's hard for me to even *think* about that. They're the most important thing to me ever. And, you know, I know I've made mistakes in my life, but I own up to them, I repent, and I do the right thing in the end, no matter what. And that's what I want my children to come to understand about me.

More than anything, though, I want them to understand about the Lord. I want them to know that He will always be there for them, and that no matter how they may mess up, or follow the "wrong" path for a time, any steps that they take to be closer to the Lord's Salvation are good ones.

My father died in 1982, and I've been wanting to see him every day since. I want to thank him for never making me feel weird about my situation. 'Cause I'm telling you, I really don't know how I got here, but I have two sweet babies and a sweet wife, and I love every single day of it.

The simplest things make me stop daily and reflect on what I'm doing, compared to what I could be doing, had I chosen the "easy" path. I could have just pushed religion out of my life, but I never did. I could have chosen the gay life, and continued to ignore my actions, ignore my vulnerabilities and intimacies with life, and just keep refusing to take responsibility.

Sure, I've messed up. Sure, I've crossed the line, and sure, I'm not perfect. But that's why I persisted under the light of the Lord. With His grace, I was more able to take the tricky steps away from my inherent desires, and closer to my longer-term goals of an eternal family and an eternal, vulnerable love with a strong woman. I'm so grateful, every moment, to be where I am. There is no comparison between the life I'm now leading, and the life I otherwise would be.

There's not a single day when I don't look around and say to myself,

You see what you're doing, right? You're combing your little baby girl's hair. You're taking Ethan to his ball game.

It's so awesome to have my little six-year-old sitting on my belly in the mornings, saying, *Get up Daddy!*

The message is... no matter where one is in life's journey, do what you can to be closer to the Light of God's Love. Read something that will bring you into what the Heavenly Father has in store for us all. And if you are struggling with *anything* in your life that you want to change, be teachable and not defiant, and God will put the right people in your path to help you. If you want to get to the Temple, make changes and start making it happen. If you experience same sex attraction, you can still get to the Temple if you want.

Again, if Joseph Smith saw what he said he saw, there really is no other choice. *You can do it now!* [A quote from President Uchtdorf, member of the First Presidency]. And you can still keep the Liza Minnelli CD's. It's OK. I've still got mine.

Exercise a particle of faith. (Alma 32:27)

A mere, willing heart, and a desire to believe, can open the right doors, and bring us back to the presence of our Father through His Son…. At least, if we are willing to put aside our p-flags and other superficial struggles. But as you make progress, expect The Adversary to attempt to intervene. When he does and the phone rings, **_Don't Answer!!_**

I will end with a quote from Ezra Taft Benson, 13th President of the Church:

"Nothing is going to startle us more when we pass through the veil to the other side, than to realize how well we know our Father and how familiar his face is to us."

("Jesus Christ—Gifts and Expectations," in _Speeches of the Year, 1974._)

My dad has been dead now for thirty-five years and I want to see him pretty badly sometimes. If what President Benson said is true, that must mean I will want to see my Father in Heaven as badly as my earthly father. And I just have to keep trying, and use Christ's atonement throughout my life, to get in to see my Father.

And someday, when I run into my ancestor Abraham Berry, who was shot in the back protecting the missionaries down in

Mississippi, what will I say? Hopefully that I did my best, and that I want in to see my Father.

I want in. Along with my wife and kids. *I want in.*

Dear Readers,

I am grateful for the opportunity to share my thoughts, and, as well, a few experiences pertaining to Keith's book.

I must admit that when Keith told me he wanted to write a book about his life, I was nervous about the whole idea. I wasn't sure what to expect. We'd had a horrible year, and all I wanted was to move forward and keep the past in the past. Little did I know that, through the process of writing the book, our marriage would become stronger than ever before. And now, having read his story, I can only say that my love for him has deepened. He is the love of my life. My dearest friend. My eternal companion.

Some might wonder what compelled me to marry someone with such a colorful past. I can truly say it was divine intervention. I can look back and see how the Lord was gradually preparing the way for Keith to enter my life. I remember when, after about a month or so of communicating online, I was reading a message he'd sent me. I don't recall what he said, but I clearly remember addressing my Heavenly Father and saying to Him, *please don't let this be some gay guy who just wants to ride my skirt-tail all the way to the Temple.*

Then, a few weeks before his first visit, I opened an email from Keith, and there it was: his sordid past in black and white. I was stunned! How do you reply to news like that? I didn't know what to do. So I knelt by my bed, and asked my Heavenly Father for guidance. I can't tell you how long I was there, praying, but it was hours. Then it happened. A feeling of love and peace washed over me. I knew without a doubt the Lord had already forgiven Keith for his past transgressions. His desire for an eternal family was genuine. This was meant to be. He was the one I'd been waiting for.

We shared many wonderful experiences throughout our lives together. But, no one can predict the future. Life is a roller coaster, filled with ups and downs, twists and turns. But it's not about the ride, it's about the way we navigate through the ride. I knew when something was off. Keith wasn't his normal self. But, then again, our lives hadn't been normal since my illness.

I never could have anticipated what was revealed to me that day. I know there were some who thought I should have left Keith for what he did; the family surrounding us considered his sin unforgivable. But there is no sin unforgivable in the eyes of our Lord, so long as we are willing to repent. We all sin, and we all have the choice to repent. Let me share with you some scripture from the book of John, chapter 8: 3-7:

3 And the scribes and Pharisees brought unto him a woman taken in adultery; and when they had set her in the midst,

4 They say unto him, Master, this woman was taken in adultery, in the very act.

5 Now Moses in the law commanded us, that such should be stoned: but what sayest thou?

6 This they said, tempting him, that they might have to accuse him. But Jesus stooped down, and with his finger wrote on the ground, as though he heard them not.

7 So when they continued asking him, he lifted up himself, and said unto them, He that is without sin among you, let him first cast a stone at her.

I won't deny, I was angry, hurt, and I wanted him to feel the pain I was feeling. My heart was broken. I'd been betrayed. The physical and emotional pain was almost unbearable. As Keith mentioned, I clawed at my arms: until they were hurt and bleeding. But I welcomed the pain. I wanted to feel anything other than the pain that was in my heart. I wanted to get even; find someone to fool around with… I figured, maybe, then, he'd know how it felt. But that's not me. My mother always said, *two wrongs don't make a right!*

This was not about evening a score. This was not about revenge. This was a battle against Satan. And I was not about to let him destroy my family. Keith is a good man, who made a bad decision, during a stressful time in his life. Just because a mistake was made, it is not grounds to erase all the great and selfless things he's done in the past.

This is the man who stood by my side during each and every fertility appointment. The man who works tirelessly to provide for his family. The man who nursed me back to health when sepsis almost took my life. This is the man I love. The father of my children. And above all, he is the man who I have chosen to spend eternity with. One does not throw away their fine silver just because it becomes tarnished. It takes a little polish and hard work, but soon enough it's the beautiful silver it once was. That's what's so amazing about repentance: we, too, can be renewed. It hasn't been easy, but with some work and lots of prayer, we made it through this trial together. And together, we can we can conquer whatever lies ahead.

With gratitude,

Brenda

ACKNOWLEDGEMENTS:

To Linda Welch, my seminary teacher throughout high school, for her sweet testimony. Miss Linda would always pour out her heart to us through the scriptures. I was so drawn in; I really *listened* when she spoke, and for that I will always think of her with love in my heart.

Also, to Darren, the only person who could've gotten me out of Dallas, and on to Hawaii where I found my focus!

To Keira Faer, my fearless editor.

To my aunts Fay McLain and Betty Garrett Shepard, whom I love with all my heart.

And lastly, but most importantly, to my incredible family: for their endless support and understanding throughout this process.

ABOUT THE AUTHOR:

Keith Ivy is a carefree, fun-loving father of two, an amateur surfer, exercise nut and budding genealogist. He is, as well, a registered nurse, and loves going to work to help others through their own trials. He doesn't like to stand in the way of others' happiness, and more than anything loves spending time with his children.

This book is for them, so they can come to know their father from his own perspective, and for his wife Brenda, to come to understand who he was before they said, "I do". This book is, also, for each one of you who finds some light in the embrace of God's love, and never backs down from one of life's trials. The only way to the eternal covenant is through the walkway of God's love. And the only way to embrace God's love is by embracing yourself, for who you are.